Minnesota Railroads

Minnesota Railroads

A Photographic History, 1940–2012

STEVE GLISCHINSKI

University of Minnesota Press
Minneapolis • London

This publication was made possible in part by the people of Minnesota through a grant funded by an appropriation to the Minnesota Historical Society from the Minnesota Arts and Cultural Heritage Fund. Any views, findings, opinions, conclusions, or recommendations expressed in this publication are those of the author and do not necessarily represent those of the State of Minnesota, the Minnesota Historical Society, or the Minnesota Historic Resources Advisory Committee.

Frontispiece: Passenger locomotives of the Rock Island and Milwaukee Road meet just west of the St. Paul Union Depot on July 25, 1969. The Rock Island diesel is pulling the last run of the Rock's *Plainsman* passenger train from Minneapolis to Kansas City, Missouri. Photograph by Byron D. Olsen.

Photograph on p. vi: On September 2, 2009, a Minnesota Northern train crosses a field near Salol. Photograph by Steve Glischinski.

Published by the University of Minnesota Press
111 Third Avenue South, Suite 290
Minneapolis, MN 55401-2520
http://www.upress.umn.edu

Library of Congress Cataloging-in-Publication Data
Glischinski, Steve.
    Minnesota railroads : a photographic history, 1940–2012 / Steve Glischinski.
    Includes bibliographical references and index.
    ISBN 978-0-8166-7591-3 (hc : alk. paper)
    ISBN 978-0-8166-7592-0 (pb : alk. paper)
1. Railroads—Minnesota—History. I. Title.
    TF24.M6G55 2012
    385.09776—dc23
                                                    2012008203

Printed in Canada on acid-free paper

The University of Minnesota is an equal-opportunity educator and employer.

19 18 17 16 15 14 13 12
10 9 8 7 6 5 4 3 2 1

To John C. Luecke

author, historian, friend

Contents

Author's Note
on Railroad Terminology

RAILROADING has its own terminology, which can be difficult to follow. For example, steam locomotives came in many different types and wheel arrangements. To differentiate between them, railroads used a classification system developed by Frederick Whyte, a Dutch mechanical engineer employed by the New York Central Railroad. Whyte's system describes the wheel arrangement of conventional steam locomotives: the first number is the number of leading wheels, the middle number (or numbers) gives the number and arrangement of drivers, and the last is the number of trailing wheels. A 4-8-4 is a steam locomotive that has four leading wheels, eight driving wheels, and four trailing wheels.

Steam locomotive types often had names associated with them, too. The 4-8-4, for example, was called a Northern because the first of the type was built for the Northern Pacific Railway. New York Central was the first railroad to own a 4-6-4, and because much of its main line in New York State paralleled the Hudson River, the 4-6-4 became known as a Hudson. References to steam locomotive wheel arrangements, types, and names are found throughout this book.

Diesel locomotives have their own terminology. Several diesels working together form multiple units of locomotives. There are dozens of different diesel models. General Motors Electro-Motive Division (EMD)

began building a line of streamlined E series passenger diesels in 1937. The term "E-units" refers to the model numbers given to each successive type, which all begin with *E*. The *E* originally stood for eighteen hundred horsepower, the power output of the earliest model, but the letter was kept for later models with far higher power ratings. The first types were the EA and E1, and the line continued through the popular E7, E8, and E9 models. The last one was produced in 1963.

In 1939, EMD introduced the shorter, streamlined F-unit. These popular diesels began production with the FT model and continued until 1960, when the last of sixty dual diesel and electric FL9 locomotives rolled off the assembly line for the New Haven Railroad. Originally intended for freight service, F models gained widespread use in passenger service as well. Versions of both E- and F-units were built without cabs; these were booster, or B-units. A-units were engines with cabs. A railroad could have a train led by an A-unit followed by any number of B-units and even more A-units. Chicago Great Western became famous for running long strings of F-units with two cabs on either end of several boosters. If five F-units were put together with cabs on each end and three boosters in between, that was an A-B-B-B-A formation. I won't try to describe every diesel model, but you will see references to the most popular types of diesels.

Acknowledgments

WRITING A BOOK can be a lonely task, with countless hours at the computer pounding out words or, in this case, combing through thousands of photographs. On this journey I am grateful for fellow travelers who helped me immeasurably.

It is traditional in book acknowledgments to thank your family last, but here they deserve top billing. My ever-patient and faithful wife, Lori, tolerated my increasing rants as deadlines drew near. She read much of the text, giving me input from a "civilian" to make sure I didn't get overly technical with my railroad terms. My son, Andy, ever the critic, looked over the photographs, giving his own thumbs-up or thumbs-down to my choices. Thanks and love to you both.

The key to an album-style book such as this is the photographs, and I had no shortage of contributors. Without them, this volume would not exist. You will see their names in the pages that follow, but here they are gathered together for the record: Perry Becker, Roger Bee, Baron Behning, Douglass A. Buell, Tom Carlson, John Cartwright, Shawn Christie, Andy Cummings, George A. Forero Jr., Gene Hetherington, Jerry Huddleston, Aaron Isaacs, Chris Laskowski, Chuck LaVallee, John Leopard, John C. Luecke, Mark R. Lynn, Todd Mavec, Charles B. McCreary, Nathan Molldrem, Gary Nelson, Stuart J. Nelson,

Byron D. Olsen, Frank E. Sandberg Jr., David C. Schauer, Jeff Terry, Richard E. Thompson, and Harold K. Vollrath.

This book began as a way to show off the many photographs in the files of the Minnesota Historical Society that contain railroad subjects. It quickly grew beyond that narrow scope, but the contributions of the Minnesota Historical Society to this work, and the preservation of these photographs, are gratefully acknowledged.

The *Minneapolis Star Tribune* newspaper donated numerous original negatives to the Minnesota Historical Society. The newspaper staff generously allowed me and University of Minnesota Press staff to look through its archives to find prints before heading to the historical society to track down the original negatives.

The Lake Superior Railroad Museum and its staff, including curator Tim Schandel and executive director Ken Buehler, allowed me to plow through its photo files and select whatever I wanted. Railroad historian and magazine columnist Jeff Terry accompanied me on trips to Duluth and also scanned many of the photographs in this book.

Patricia Maus, curator of the Northern Minnesota Historical Center, dug through the center's collection to find a photograph of the Duluth Union Depot. The Museum of the Rockies in Bozeman, Montana, kindly allowed the use of several photographs taken or collected by the late Northern Pacific historian Ronald V. Nixon.

Helping with fact-checking and mapping was the ever-patient Pete Briggs of Briggs Business Communication. Pete has a wealth of knowledge not only about the railroad industry but also about how the railroads promoted themselves; he was previously employed in the public relations departments of the Burlington Route and its successor Burlington Northern.

Aaron Isaacs has been a great mentor as I compiled this book. He was an invaluable resource, constantly pulling photographs from his own collection and giving me access to the collections of the Minnesota Streetcar Museum and Joe Elliott's fine work. The coauthor of *Twin Cities by Trolley: The Streetcar Era in Minneapolis and St. Paul,* Aaron encouraged me to work with the University of Minnesota Press.

Do you have a question about the Soo Line Railroad? The man to answer it is Stuart J. Nelson. Stu grew up in a railroad family and went to work for the Soo Line at a young age. Over the course of decades he amassed an incredible amount of information and history about his favorite railroad. His recall and ability to quickly check facts pertaining to the Soo are amazing. He showed patience and generosity in answering dozens of e-mail queries from me, for which I am grateful.

A special acknowledgment must go to the late William D. Middleton, one of the giants of railroad

photography in the past fifty years. He had few peers among authors of railroad books: he wrote or co-wrote twenty-three volumes, many of them standards in the field. He played a leading role in the creation of the *Encyclopedia of North American Railroads,* published in 2004. I became acquainted with him when he asked me to contribute to the encyclopedia, and when I contacted him about this book, he was happy to participate. Middleton lived in Minnesota in the late 1950s. He allowed me to review his proof sheets of the many photographs he took at that time and to select any that I wanted to use. He was a kind and generous man whose work will live on in the thousands of expertly composed black-and-white images he created.

Equally generous was Minnesota railroad historian John C. Luecke, who has assembled an extraordinary collection of historic Minnesota railroad photographs. His attitude was "if you like it, use it." I liked what John collected and used as much as I could. Without his contributions this book would be far less comprehensive.

John and my posse of proofreaders (Jerry Huddleston, Mark Lynn, Jeff Terry, David C. Schauer, and Lori Van Oosbree) checked my information. I tried to double-check everything, but any errors in this book are mine and mine alone.

Finally, my thanks to the University of Minnesota Press for being willing to undertake the production of this book. Todd Orjala and editorial assistant Kristian Tvedten patiently endured endless questions, e-mail messages, and, of course, inevitable delays. I hope our readers find our efforts worthwhile.

Dominant, Disappearing, Reborn:
Seventy Years of Minnesota Railroad History

WHEN I WAS YOUNG, my father (who worked his entire career at Northwest Airlines but was fascinated by railroads) took my brother and me to watch trains. Our favorite location was along Warner Road just east of downtown St. Paul along the cliffs of Dayton's Bluff. We spent many happy hours there, watching trains of the Burlington, Chicago & North Western, Rock Island, and especially the Chicago, Milwaukee, St. Paul & Pacific, nicknamed Milwaukee Road. The highlight of any evening at the Bluff was the last passenger train of the day—at least for us, since we had to get home to bed. That was the Milwaukee Road's *Fast Mail*. As it departed the St. Paul Union Depot and approached our location, the engineer throttled up the locomotives as he accelerated the train out of the city. It was quite a sight: a single coach and a long line of mail and railway post office cars with men visible in the windows sorting the mail. After it roared away we would head home with visions of speeding trains in our heads.

For some reason, an interest in trains and railroading stuck with me. While my father and brother maintained a casual interest in railroading, I became what my wife bluntly terms obsessed. In 1970 I bought a Kodak Instamatic camera and began taking photographs of trains, using my bike to travel ever-farther distances in Minneapolis and St. Paul to see different railroads. In 1972 my parents gave me a 35 mm camera and I began shooting slides. The next year, with a driver's license and access to a car, my horizons expanded further. I joined a few railroad clubs and was able to meet other people with a similar obsession, er, interest.

Many in the railroad groups of the early 1970s had a nonchalant attitude. The steam engines and passenger trains they had grown up with were gone, and so were many of the railroads. The Burlington Northern merger had recently occurred, taking with it the Burlington, Great Northern, and Northern Pacific, the favorite roads of many. They simply could not comprehend why I would want to go out and take pictures of contemporary railroading. "Why do you bother?" they would say. "All the neat stuff is gone, and everything today looks the same."

I hadn't been around for steam, and I found Amtrak to be an exciting enterprise as it tried to revive passenger service. I kept on taking pictures, and eventually some were published in magazines such as *Trains*. I was always the youngest guy in our railroad groups, and eventually I started to amass a large collection of railroad slides. By the 1980s and 1990s, I was no longer the youngest guy, and another change occurred: people began to appreciate the photographs I had taken when I first started out. I distinctly remember one railroad fan saying to a friend of mine, "He's got some really cool stuff from the 1970s!"

The lesson wasn't lost on me. Many things had changed, and somewhat by accident others and I had been documenting those changes in photographs. Railroads merged, lines were abandoned, different paint schemes came and went, museums were started, and even a few steam locomotives were put back in service for special runs. The pace of change was so fast we could barely keep up. Yet most of this change was barely noticed by the public. With the end of passenger train service, railroads were perceived as a dying industry—which indeed it was during much of the 1960s and 1970s. The only contact many people had with railroading was at a railroad crossing, and they were usually annoyed if they had to wait for a train.

That's a shame, because Minnesota was once a center of railroad activity, serving as the jumping-off point for the transcontinental railroads Great North-

ern, Milwaukee Road, and Northern Pacific, home to midsized railroads Minneapolis & St. Louis and Soo Line, and headquarters for iron-ore carrier Duluth, Missabe and Iron Range, which moved some of the heaviest trains in the world.

While the public wasn't looking, railroads returned from the brink of oblivion and are now in the forefront of transportation success and innovation. Legislation that partially deregulated railroads was backed by the Carter administration and passed in 1980. Coupled with ever-increasing demand for western coal to provide fuel for U.S. power plants, this resulted in a remarkable renaissance of railroading. Throughout the 1980s and 1990s lines were rebuilt, new equipment was ordered, and larger profits were made. I look back at slides I took at Dayton's Bluff in the 1970s and see weedy, uneven track and roadbed. The same area today has heavy welded rail, new signaling systems, and nary a weed in sight.

The U.S. rail industry is in better physical condition than ever and, in contrast to other businesses, survived the economic downturn that began in 2007 almost as if it never happened. Railroad traffic dropped 20 to 30 percent but profits did not, and railroads continued to spend billions of dollars to prepare their infrastructure for the inevitable economic comeback. Today's welded rail and concrete ties enable railroads to handle heavy trains and heavily loaded cars far better than during World War II, the starting point for this book. While airlines struggle to make a profit as fuel prices bounce up and down, railroads have maintained a steady, profitable course. Railroads are even "green." New diesel locomotives are so efficient that railroads use about the same amount of fuel as they did twenty years ago while hauling almost double the amount of freight.

This revival has gone largely unnoticed, outside of Wall Street investors and industry insiders. The public is so misinformed that when debates were raging about President Obama's plans for high-speed rail, it was derided as "old technology"—as if technology that has been proven efficient and profitable for more than a century was somehow a bad thing.

Minnesota Railroads documents in photographs the many changes in Minnesota railroading in the past seventy years, a period many railroad fans consider railroading's most colorful era. During this time the largest technological change in railroad history occurred: the transition from external combustion steam locomotives to internal combustion diesel locomotives. In the 1940s and 1950s, modern steam locomotives and new diesels rode the rails, creating a colorful variety of trains not seen before or since. During the same period, new streamlined passenger trains entered service clad in colorful paint schemes that expressed the optimism of the railroads after the busy years of World War II. Then came the twin crushing blows of the interstate highway system and the expansion of air travel, which killed passenger train service and cut into freight traffic as well, followed by the industry's revival in the 1980s and 1990s and into the twenty-first century.

This book is a salute to railroad history but also recognizes that railroading is here to stay. While looking through these pages, bear in mind that despite the colorful and fascinating past of railroads, their best days may still be to come.

Through all the ups and downs, Minnesota's railroads have been and remain wonderful subjects for photography. As old locomotives worked alongside new, as tracks were abandoned or rebuilt, as old railroad names departed the scene and new ones took their place, skilled photographers documented the changes on film and with digital cameras. The result of their efforts is found on the pages of *Minnesota Railroads: A Photographic History, 1940–2012.*

This is the view from the control tower at the east end of the St. Paul Union Depot on the morning of September 29, 1948. On the left is Burlington Route's *Morning Zephyr* headed for Chicago. The streamliner received Vista Dome cars in 1947—the first in the country to feature the glass-topped cars. On the right is what appears to be either a special train with Pullman sleeping cars or the overnight *Black Hawk* from Chicago. The new E7 diesel on the train sports painted grills next to the headlight meant to resemble the grills on the shovel-nosed diesel on the *Morning Zephyr*. Barely visible under the sheds to the left are the wheels of a steam locomotive. Photograph by *St. Paul Dispatch–Pioneer Press*, Minnesota Historical Society Collection.

1

An Industry in Transition

1940–1960

"THE GREAT NORTHERN RAILWAY, in the eventful year of 1941, met every requirement made of it as the Nation hurriedly prepared for war. As this is written, well along in the following year, that record still holds. For the railroad is the beginning and the backbone of the assembly lines from which eventually roll the tanks, airplanes, guns, munitions and the other requirements of our armed forces. Any interruption of railway transportation and the whole assembly line would stop. War production would be paralyzed. Our responsibility is clear and grave. Come what may, there must be no interruption."

These are the words of Frank J. Gavin, president of the Great Northern Railway, in 1942.[1] The Great Northern was a prosperous railroad based in St. Paul, one of several railroad companies with headquarters in Minnesota. In 1941 Great Northern operated 1,108 miles of main line and 978 miles of branch lines in the state, making it Minnesota's largest railroad. Gavin

was directing his words to Great Northern employees, but he could have been speaking for every Minnesota railroad as they struggled with huge volumes of freight and passengers during the war.

The two decades from 1940 to 1960 were a time of incredible change for the railroads of Minnesota and of the nation. Railroad traffic surged as never before because of World War II and then plummeted so that by 1960 railroads seemed irrelevant, at least to the general public. Railroads were a dominant industry in the 1940s, vital to the successful war effort. They transported the majority of intercity travelers and had the largest market share in transporting freight. The public had a close connection to railroads. In addition to riding trains, rare was the family that didn't have at least one relative employed in the railroad industry.

Following the war and into the 1950s, railroads reequipped passenger trains on major routes and

1

began the wholesale replacement of steam locomotives with diesel locomotives that cost less to operate. However, by the end of the 1950s the railroad industry was heading for serious trouble; it wouldn't recover until the 1980s and 1990s.

Not many would have predicted such a bleak future during the war years of the 1940s. The long slide in railroad passenger traffic, which began in the 1920s and continued into the following decade, was suddenly arrested with the advent of World War II. During the war, troop movements and restrictions on automobile fuel generated a huge increase in passenger traffic from the low point of the Depression 1930s. For example, in 1940, the number of revenue passenger miles (calculated by multiplying the total number of revenue-paying passengers aboard a train by the distance traveled in miles) of Minnesota railroads was 260,897,000. In 1945, revenue passenger train miles in Minnesota reached 984,633,000.[2]

Although the increase in passengers during the war brought prosperity to the railroads, it didn't last, thanks largely to the automobile. Americans began acquiring cars en masse as far back as the 1920s. In 1916 there were only 3 million motor vehicles registered in the United States, but by 1929 there were 23 million. Railroads carried 1 billion passengers in 1920;[3] by 1930 this had dropped to 700 million; it slid to 450 million by 1940.[4] World War II stopped the decline as a flood of war-related passenger and freight traffic came to the the railroads, but with the end of hostilities in 1945, more and more people abandoned passenger trains for the comfort and convenience of the private automobile.

Railroads were optimistic that people would still ride their trains. They thought the public would not want to drive long distances, especially on substandard roads. They spent millions to reequip their passenger trains for the anticipated postwar demand—a decision *Classic Trains Magazine* called a "magnificent miscalculation" since passenger business had been on that long downward trend before World War II, even with new streamlined trains and faster schedules. That trend continued with the end of hostilities, but the railroads failed to recognize it.

The Great Northern planned for the expected postwar boom. In 1943 the company announced it was spending $7 million for five twelve-car train sets and ten locomotives for an all-new, streamlined *Empire Builder* for delivery when the war ended. The *Empire Builder* was Great Northern's flagship train from Chicago to the Pacific Northwest. It was named in honor of James J. Hill (1838–1916), founder of the Great Northern, who had called St. Paul his home. It used the rails of the Chicago, Burlington & Quincy (Burlington Route), jointly owned by Great Northern and Northern Pacific, from Chicago to the St. Paul Union Depot, where it switched to Great Northern rails. Rival railroads Milwaukee Road and Northern Pacific also ordered new cars for their transcontinental trains, the *Olympian Hiawatha* and *North Coast Limited,* respectively, on routes roughly parallel to Great Northern's. The Burlington Route bought the first dome cars for the Chicago–Twin Cities *Twin Zephyrs* in December 1947. The Milwaukee Road built its own cars to reequip its Chicago–Minneapolis/St. Paul *Twin Cities Hiawathas* that entered service on May 29, 1948.

Even with the new trains, passenger business kept trending downward. In 1944, 74 percent of intercity travel was by rail. By 1949 this had fallen to 48 percent, and it dropped to 29 percent by 1960.[5] The lure of the open road, especially as federal and state governments subsidized new road construction, enticed travelers away from the rails. Following World War II, Ford and General Motors turned from war production back to building cars and trucks. This coincided with low-cost gasoline and a push for modern highways, which culminated in the National Interstate and Defense Highways Act of 1956. The act authorized the construction of the interstate highway system, which was a severe blow to passenger rail service. Why wait for the train when you can have the freedom to set your own schedule? The new roads were enjoyed not only by automobiles but also by trucks, the main competition for freight hauled by rail. By the 1960s less-than-carload freight—small package freight—had virtually vanished from the rails.[6]

In the 1940s and 1950s another formidable threat appeared: affordable commercial aviation. Government entities built sprawling urban and suburban airports, funded construction of highways to provide access to them, and provided air traffic control services. As aviation became more practical as a travel option, more travelers took advantage of the speed of the airliner. In 1957 airplanes carried more passengers than railroads for the first time in the United States.[7]

Railroads across the nation were undergoing a technological change of massive proportions in the 1940s and 1950s: the switch from steam to diesel power. Since the beginning of the railroad industry in the 1830s, steam had been the dominant form of motive power. Rudimentary efforts to produce internal combustion locomotives began as early as 1913

with Minnesota's Dan Patch Electric Lines. That year the railroad purchased gasoline-electric locomotive 100 from General Electric for freight service, the first of its kind ever built. Together with gas-electric self-propelled motor cars carrying passengers, Dan Patch Lines made history as the first railroad operating exclusively with gasoline-electric equipment.[8] Other Minnesota railroads such as Northern Pacific and Minneapolis & St. Louis also used gas-electrics in passenger service beginning in the 1920s and 1930s, but these small efforts at internal combustion motive power scarcely made a dent in an era when the steam locomotive reigned supreme.

It wasn't until the 1930s and the advent of streamliners that the diesel locomotive caught the attention of the railroads. Electro-Motive Corporation (originally called Electro-Motive Engineering and founded in 1922) began production of diesel engines for streamlined trains. General Motors had purchased the company in 1930 along with its engine supplier, Winton Engine. With production facilities in La Grange, Illinois, Electro-Motive in the 1930s built high-quality, reliable locomotives that were successful with railroads across the nation, mainly in passenger service.

Electro-Motive garnered more business when it sent a new freight locomotive on a barnstorming tour to convince railroads of the efficiency of freight diesel locomotives. Electro-Motive 103, the first successful road freight diesel, brought sales victory for Electro-Motive and doom for the steam locomotive. No. 103 weighed 900,000 pounds and produced 5,400 horsepower from its four diesel units. From November 1939 to October 1940, it pulled freight trains in thirty-five states, including Minnesota, over the lines of twenty Class 1 railroads.[9] No. 103 proved to be faster and more efficient than any steam locomotive then operating and convinced many railroads that the time of the diesel had come. In 1941 Electro-Motive Corporation was renamed the Electro-Motive Division of General Motors, commonly referred to simply as EMD. It led the charge to convert America's railroads to diesel power, a process that accelerated following World War II and was essentially complete by 1960.

The transition from steam to diesel ultimately was a business and technological success for the railroads, but it exacted a heavy economic and social toll on many communities. In the steam era, railroads set up division points approximately every one hundred miles, where steam locomotives were serviced, trains switched, and crews changed. Most division points had roundhouses for working on steam locomotives, and some cities, such as Brainerd and Two Harbors, had large shop facilities to service and rebuild them. Diesel locomotives were less labor-intensive and didn't have to stop for coal or water. In the 1950s steam roundhouses and shops were closed. Diesels also required fewer crew members—for example, there no longer was a need for a fireman, although it would take several years for the fireman's position to be eliminated. Railroad workers who had built their careers around steam locomotives suddenly found themselves without employment, and this effect rippled through railroad towns of the state.

In northern Minnesota, two entirely new railroads came on the scene in the 1950s. They were constructed to move taconite, a low-grade type of iron ore. When higher-grade natural iron ore was plentiful, taconite was considered a waste rock and not used. As the supply of high-grade natural ore decreased, especially after World War II, the steel industry began to view taconite as a resource. Dr. E. W. Davis of the University of Minnesota, along with other scientists and engineers, conducted years of tests and experiments to find a way to take the iron ore out of the taconite rock. After many years of research, a process was developed to create taconite pellets. Taconite literally saved Minnesota's iron ore mining industry.

In 1955, Reserve Mining Company opened a private forty-seven-mile railroad from its mining area at the new town of Babbitt to a taconite processing plant at Silver Bay. Silver Bay was built from scratch by the company on the North Shore of Lake Superior and was home to approximately 3,500 workers and their families. Reserve, the first successful large-scale taconite mining operation in Minnesota, hauled raw ore from Babbitt to Silver Bay in thirty-foot-long open-top ore cars. By 1957, the Silver Bay plant was producing 5 million tons of taconite pellets per year, which required the railroad to move 15 million tons of raw taconite ore over the railroad. The operation was so successful that the single-track railroad was double-tracked in 1961.[10]

Erie Mining Company opened a new taconite plant at Hoyt Lakes in September 1957, and like Reserve, Erie built its own railroad. Erie's pellet-processing plant was at the west end of the railroad; rather than moving raw ore, it hauled finished taconite pellets seventy-four miles to a new ore dock at Taconite Harbor on Lake Superior. There the pellets were dumped into the holds of lake boats for movement to the blast furnaces of the East and Midwest. A loop track at Taconite Harbor allowed entire trains to turn and head back to the Hoyt Lakes plant without ever uncoupling. Erie also built an extensive railroad in the mining areas at Hoyt Lakes. Trains dumped raw ore in a central crusher building. Both the Erie and Reserve operations took place in sparsely populated territory: in 1968, less than one person per square mile lived in the area traversed by Reserve's railroad.[11]

By 1960, diesels had taken over from steam, the passenger train was in severe decline, and long-haul truckers were eating into the railroads' freight business. The long decline would not be arrested until the 1980s. Railroads chafed under government regulation and obtained no largesse from the government even as roads and aviation received large subsidies. In the 1960s and 1970s, these problems boiled to the surface with mergers, bankruptcies, and the government takeover of rail passenger service with Amtrak.

Despite looming problems, the two decades from 1940 to 1960 were exciting times for Minnesota railroading. Heavy freight and passenger traffic, new streamliners and diesels, the two new iron ore railroads, and long trains pulled by powerful steam locomotives were all part of the mix. In the 1950s as the steam locomotive disappeared, railroad fans organized trips to bid them farewell. It was the last hurrah before railroading moved out of the public consciousness and slipped into the background of American life.

All the elements of classic steam-era railroading are present in this photograph taken outside the St. Paul Union Depot on May 30, 1948. A Burlington Route train is arriving from Chicago, likely the *Black Hawk*. Hudson-type locomotive 3004 is up front as the train passes the Union Depot roundhouse and under Kellogg Boulevard. This train is virtually identical to what it was in the 1920s, but changes are on the way in the form of streamlined cars and diesel locomotives. Indeed, to the right are diesels of competitor Milwaukee Road. The biggest change will be the decline of passenger service—in a little over two decades the Union Depot will close, a thought no doubt unimaginable to the railroaders in this scene. Photograph by Sid Davies; collection of John C. Luecke.

Viewed from farther up the tracks, two trains are captured in the summer of 1954. On the right is Northern Pacific train 12 from International Falls, due into the depot at 7:15 a.m. On the left is Chicago Great Western train 14 from Omaha leaving for Minneapolis, where it is scheduled to arrive at 7:35 a.m. The Chicago Great Western in later years wasn't a major passenger carrier; trains from the Twin Cities served Kansas City and Omaha on slower schedules with older equipment. They were primarily local trains serving the small towns along the "Corn Belt Route," as the Chicago Great Western advertised itself. Photograph by Charles B. McCreary.

[ABOVE] Chicago & North Western subsidiary Chicago, St. Paul, Minneapolis & Omaha (Omaha Road) lived in the shadow of the Chicago & North Western as a semi-independent line. Most of its 1,700 miles of track were in Wisconsin and Minnesota, but there was additional track in Iowa, Nebraska, and South Dakota. In August 1948 Omaha Road 4-6-2 No. 602 is steaming east with a train for Chicago. Collection of Tim Schandel.

[BELOW] On a summer morning in 1954, the observation car of Rock Island's *Zephyr-Rocket* slips into the station at 7:10 a.m. after an overnight trip from St. Louis. After a brief stop it will continue on to the Milwaukee Road station in Minneapolis. The Burlington Route operated the train from St. Louis to Burlington, Iowa, where it was handed off to the Rock Island. Great Northern diesels are heading to the roundhouse for servicing after bringing the *Empire Builder* into the station from the West Coast. Photograph by Charles B. McCreary.

The interior of the Union Depot concourse is seen on July 1, 1949. The concourse is a huge space: eighty feet wide and three hundred feet long, spanning nine platforms. Passengers reached their trains through gates on the east side of the concourse using stairs, and later escalators and elevators. Wood fixtures at the gates identified the track number, destination, and departure or arrival time of the train on the track below.

Little noticed by travelers are bas-relief sculptures over the brick archways that depict the development of transportation from wagon train to locomotive. The skylights in the concourse were blacked out during World War II but are being restored as part of a multimillion-dollar restoration begun in 2011. Minnesota Historical Society Collection.

This aerial view shows the extent of the Union Depot facilities with its nine platforms and eighteen tracks. It was built and owned by the Saint Paul Union Depot Company, a Minnesota corporation owned in equal shares by the railroads whose passenger trains served St. Paul. Its management was independent and responsible for the operation and financing of the facility, including the buildings, tracks, platforms, umbrella sheds, and switching locomotives. Charges to participating railroads went toward debt service, operations, and maintenance. This view was taken in March 1968, but the building is identical to how it appeared in the 1940s. Note that the Lafayette freeway bridge was under construction at the time. Photograph by Robert McCoy; collection of Nathan Molldrem.

[ABOVE] On the west side of the depot, as seen from the Robert Street Bridge, Milwaukee Road 14A and 14B are switching out mail and express cars before departing for Minneapolis. The two diesels are model DL109s built by American Locomotive Company in October 1941. Only seventy-eight DL109s were built between December 1939 and April 1945. They were styled by noted industrial designer Otto Kuhler, who incorporated an unusual three-piece windshield into his design. Author's collection.

[BELOW] After the passenger train departs, a Milwaukee Road freight train steams past the depot heading for Minneapolis. The use of two engines, referred to as doubleheading, were necessary for Short Line Hill, a steep grade that began just west of the depot and continued for approximately five miles to Snelling Avenue in St. Paul. This view was recorded from the Robert Street Bridge. Author's collection.

[ABOVE] Unlike St. Paul, Minneapolis had two large downtown passenger terminals, the Great Northern Station on Hennepin Avenue and the Milwaukee Road Depot a few blocks east on Washington, both designed by Charles S. Frost, who was also the architect of the St. Paul Union Depot. The Milwaukee Road Depot opened in 1899 and served trains of the Milwaukee Road, Rock Island, and Soo Line. A distinctive feature of the depot is its block-long train shed along Washington Avenue, which sheltered passengers from the elements. Milwaukee Road's *Afternoon Hiawatha* to Chicago is under the shed in 1965. Photograph by Byron D. Olsen.

[RIGHT] The Milwaukee's Road's *Hiawatha* began service between the Twin Cities and Chicago in 1935 with steam locomotives. Diesels were first used in 1941, with much fanfare. Prior to the departure of the *Morning Hiawatha* from Minneapolis on September 20, 1941, Janet Lowell, the only female member of the Twin City Chapter of the Diesel Locomotive Fans Association, christened the new Hiawatha diesels. A bottle of water from Minnehaha Falls was used. Shown at the ceremony are, on the left, Miss Lowell; D. T. Bagnell, superintendent of the Milwaukee Road's La Crosse & River Division; and E. F. Conway, Minneapolis captain of police. The men on the right are Carl Frank, electrician; M. S. Huber, locomotive engineer; and William Sukau, diesel maintainer for the Electro-Motive. The diesel, a two-unit model E6, came to be known as *Famous 15* because it racked up an amazing record of service. No. 15 would pull the overnight *Fast Mail* from Chicago to Minneapolis and, after slightly more than a ninety-minute layover, would pull the *Morning Hiawatha* back to Chicago, frequently at speeds in excess of one hundred miles per hour. The locomotive held this assignment from 1941 to 1949 with rarely a day off. Photograph by *Minneapolis Star Tribune*, Minnesota Historical Society Collection.

THE MILWAUKEE ROAD

[LEFT] At the Milwaukee Road Depot on May 27, 1948, visitors are touring the new cars for the twice-daily *Twin Cities Hiawatha* streamliners between Minneapolis/St. Paul and Chicago. To introduce them to the public, they were sent on tour so prospective passengers could "kick the tires" of the new trains. Open for viewing at the rear of the new train was the distinctive Skytop lounge observation car. Noted industrial designer Brooks Stevens, who also created the Miller Brewing logo and the Oscar Mayer Wienermobile, created the Skytop design. The four cars were built by the railroad at the Milwaukee shops, and with their huge glass area they were unlike any other railroad passenger car. One Skytop remains in operating condition and is based in Minneapolis. The *Twin Cities Hiawatha* entered service two days after this photograph was taken. Photograph by *Minneapolis Star Journal,* Minnesota Historical Society Collection.

[OPPOSITE, ABOVE] The Skytop lounge observation cars were replacements for another distinctive Milwaukee Road observation car, the Beaver Tails of 1938. Like the Skytops, they were built at the Milwaukee shops. Four cars were constructed for use on the reequipped *Hiawatha* that entered service September 19, 1938. They featured two large windows at the rear, with a rear-facing sofa on the interior. Exterior fins shaded the windows for easier viewing, and ribbed sides gave the cars a distinctive look. In January 1939, Milwaukee Road inaugurated the *Morning Hiawatha;* the original train was renamed the *Afternoon Hiawatha.* On October 13, 1946, a Beaver Tail brings up the rear of the *Afternoon Hiawatha* departing Red Wing. Photograph by Ronald V. Nixon, Museum of the Rockies Photo Archive.

[OPPOSITE, BELOW] In August 1948, the two-month-old *Afternoon Hiawatha* shows off its new equipment as it races along the Mississippi River near River Junction in La Crescent. The train will head east at the junction, cross the Mississippi River, and pause at the depot in La Crosse, Wisconsin, before continuing its race to the Windy City. The Milwaukee Road main line paralleled the Mississippi for 129 miles from St. Paul Union Depot to La Crosse. Photograph by Charles B. McCreary.

Viewed from the top of Barn Bluff in Red Wing, the majesty of the Mississippi River Valley is on display as a westbound mail and express train arrives on July 9, 1947. The steam locomotive is a streamlined 4-6-4 F7-class Hudson. Designer Otto Kuhler styled the shrouding with orange and gray paint and silver wings. Six Hudsons were built by American Locomotive in 1938 for heavy high-speed passenger service. They once pulled glamour trains such as the *Hiawatha*s, but by 1947 diesels had taken over many runs and the beautiful engines wound up on secondary trains such as this. Photograph by Ronald V. Nixon, Museum of the Rockies Photo Archive.

[LEFT] In February 1952, Milwaukee Road 261 brings a passenger train through St. Paul near Pleasant Avenue. At that time it was one of hundreds of anonymous steam locomotives on the Milwaukee Road. No. 261 was donated to the National Railroad Museum in Green Bay, Wisconsin, in 1956. In 1992 it was leased and moved to Minneapolis, where it was restored to operation the following year. In 1995 the nonprofit Friends of the 261 assumed operation of the locomotive and in 2010 purchased it from the museum. Still based in Minneapolis, 261 pulls periodic excursions trips around Minnesota and the Midwest. Photograph by James Kreuzberger, Minnesota Streetcar Museum Collection.

[RIGHT] Railroads were the primary mode of transportation of both passengers and war material during World War II, and their advertising played up the theme of patriotism. This notebook from 1945 shows a soldier and an electric Bi-Polar locomotive, which pulled the Milwaukee Road's *Olympian* over its electrified lines in Washington State. Author's collection.

Minneapolis's Great Northern Station opened in 1914 serving the Burlington, Chicago & North Western, Omaha Road, Great Northern, Northern Pacific, and Chicago Great Western. During World War I, trains of the Minneapolis & St. Louis also moved to the depot. It was constructed of brick and reinforced concrete and was faced with light Kettle River sandstone. The station tracks ran along the Mississippi River and under Hennepin Avenue. This view was taken in 1962. Photograph by Byron D. Olsen.

The waiting room of the Great Northern Station has few travelers on the afternoon of July 7, 1950. The ticket counter is at right; newspaper and magazines were sold on the opposite side of the room. Above the news vendor is a large mural, a composite of scenes in Glacier National Park, served by Great Northern. The mural depicts the yearly meeting of the Blackfeet and Kootenai Indian tribes, with a vista of Swiftcurrent Lake predominating. Great Northern modernized the station in 1966, installing false ceilings and new signage on the exterior. It served Amtrak trains from May 1, 1971, to March 1, 1978, when Amtrak moved to a new station in St. Paul's Midway area. The Great Northern Station was demolished in the summer of 1978, but Burlington Northern officials saved the mural from destruction. Photograph by *Minneapolis Star Tribune,* Minnesota Historical Society Collection.

With the Mississippi River in the foreground, Northern Pacific train 4, the *Alaskan,* departs the Great Northern Station in 1951, passing under the Third Avenue Bridge. The paint design on the front of the lo-comotive is meant to resemble a pine tree. Photograph by Charles B. McCreary.

The Minneapolis, Northfield & Southern was created in 1918 when it took over operations of the Dan Patch Electric Line between Minneapolis and Northfield. During the 1930s, Minneapolis, Northfield & Southern purchased seven used 2-10-0 type locomotives, known as Decapods. Two more came in the 1940s, including 506, here being serviced at the roundhouse at Glenwood Junction in Golden Valley in May 1948. This engine was built in 1944 for the USSR but was purchased by Minneapolis, Northfield & Southern instead. Photograph by Roy W. Carlson, from Aaron Isaacs; collection of Harold K. Vollrath.

Predating diesels and streamliners were gas-electric cars. The engine was up front followed (usually) by a baggage or railway post office compartment and coach seating. Sometimes dubbed "doodlebugs" for their ungainly appearance, they were an effort to save money over conventional steam-powered trains. An early user was the Dan Patch Electric Line and successor Minneapolis, Northfield & Southern. On April 30, 1942, the last day of Minneapolis, Northfield & Southern passenger service to Northfield, car 14 is ready to depart the Minneapolis station shared with the Minnesota Western at Third Avenue North and Seventh Street North. Photograph by *Minneapolis Star Journal*, Minnesota Historical Society Collection.

Another user of gas-electric cars was the Minneapolis & St. Louis Railway. The Minneapolis-based railroad received eleven cars between December 1929 and July 1931, eight of which were named as well as numbered. In the 1940s and 1950s the power plants on seven of the cars were replaced with diesels. Car GE-28, *Watertown,* is passing Cedar Lake Yard in Minneapolis's Kenwood neighborhood en route to Des Moines with train 2 in 1951. The car is towing one of three baggage cars rebuilt from World War II troop sleepers. Behind the baggage car is a streamlined coach, one of six received by the Louie in May 1948. Photograph by Charles B. McCreary.

Between 1924 and 1929, Northern Pacific purchased a fleet of twenty-two gas-electric rail cars from Electro-Motive Corporation, predecessor of the Electro-Motive Division of General Motors. The cars were seen as a cost-effective alternative to regular passenger trains on lightly used branch lines, mainly in Minnesota, North Dakota, and Washington. After World War II many were converted to diesel-electric operation.

As a Great Northern freight waits in the distance, car B-18 crosses the Great Northern tracks at Breckenridge on April 20, 1959. It is operating as train 112 from Oakes, North Dakota, to Staples. Car B-18 was built in January 1929 and scrapped in December 1963. Photograph by William D. Middleton.

[ABOVE] For sixty-eight years Northern Pacific maintained a twenty-mile branch line between Wyoming, Minnesota, and Taylors Falls. Noted for its scenery and high trestles in the St. Croix River Valley, service ended on June 30, 1948, when trains 725 and 726 made their final trips. With just a boxcar and coach-baggage, the trains were filled to capacity with 211 riders taking a last ride. When the combine filled, the crew opened the boxcar to passengers. At Taylors Falls, residents have turned out to see the last train. The 1902 Taylors Falls depot survives as a community center. Photograph by *Minneapolis Star,* Minnesota Historical Society Collection.

[RIGHT] To turn locomotives at Taylors Falls, the railroad installed this "armstrong" turntable in 1913, the fifth installed there. The engineer is in the process of turning Northern Pacific 328 for the return trip to Wyoming. Engine 328 was preserved and displayed at a park in Stillwater. It was restored to operation by the Minnesota Transportation Museum, which operated it in excursion service between 1981 and 1999. Author's collection.

While railroads are hesitant to acknowledge them, accidents are a fact of life in railroading. Railroading today is safer than at any time in its history, but back in the 1940s and 1950s, large crowds were drawn to wrecks to watch rescue and cleanup efforts. The crowds are thick on October 22, 1947, at the scene of a head-on collision between a North-ern Pacific freight train and a Soo Line passenger train near the Phalen Tourist Camp on St. Paul's East Side. According to the *St. Paul Dispatch*, the wreck injured more than twenty persons and drew thousands of on-lookers. Photograph by *St. Paul Dispatch* from William Briggs. Author's collection.

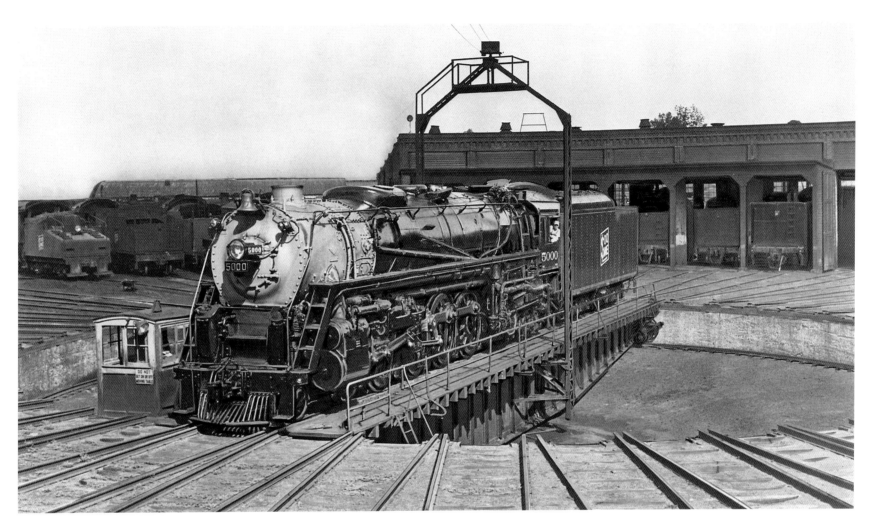

In the steam era railroads took pride in their locomotives and put their best foot forward when presenting them to the public. Soo Line published this photograph of their newest and largest steam locomotive, 4-8-4 No. 5000, posing on the turntable at Shoreham Yard in Minneapolis. The photograph has been heavily retouched to either bring out more detail or clean up an area that may have appeared less attractive. The 5000 and three sisters were built by Lima Locomotive Works in 1938 and used in fast freight service on the 452-mile run from Shoreham to Chicago. Collection of Stuart J. Nelson.

At one time railroad engineers were admired for their ability to keep huge steam locomotives under control as they roared down the tracks with fast passenger trains. While it might seem glamorous, being an engineer in the steam era was a stressful, dirty job that required working up to sixteen hours in all types of weather. Regardless of the conditions, most engineers loved their job. Great Northern engineer Huff is running 4-8-4 No. 2587 westbound near Breckenridge on the *Empire Builder* in 1945. He's decked out in the attire of the steam era: Kromer cap, bandana, and coveralls. Huff is checking over train orders that inform him of speed restrictions, meets, and other changes in operating conditions. Even though the engineer operates the locomotive, it is the conductor who is in overall charge of the train. Photograph by William J. Pontin, Rail Photo Service; collection of Gary Nelson.

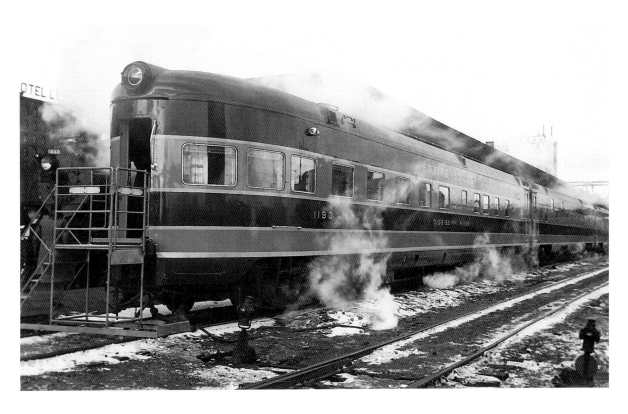

[ABOVE] In 1947, Great Northern introduced a streamlined version of the *Empire Builder*. Great Northern and partners Burlington and Spokane, Portland & Seattle spent $7 million on the train, which operated from Chicago to Seattle and Portland via Minneapolis/St. Paul. Before entering regular service, Great Northern sent the train on tour to give potential travelers a preview of the new streamliner. On February 9, 1947, it is on display at the Duluth Union Depot. Despite the cold, the door of observation car *Mississippi River* is open for visitors to see what postwar train travel is all about. The new train entered service on February 23, 1947. Photograph by James Kreuzberger, Minnesota Streetcar Museum Collection.

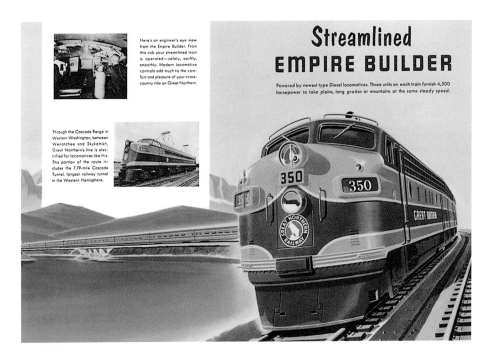

[RIGHT] Great Northern expended every effort to improve and promote the streamlined *Empire Builder*. It replaced the 1947 train with an all-new version in 1951, commonly called the "Mid-Century Empire Builder" and issued this twenty-two-page booklet that highlighted the new train's features. Author's collection.

[OPPOSITE] In the 1940s and 1950s, railroads were major employers in Minnesota. The state was home to large railroads such as Great Northern, Northern Pacific, Omaha Road, and Soo Line; midsized roads such as Duluth, Missabe & Iron Range; Duluth, Winnipeg & Pacific; and Minneapolis & St. Louis; and smaller lines such as Minneapolis, Northfield & Southern. Great Northern and Northern Pacific shared an office building in downtown St. Paul at 175 East Fourth Street. Seen here in 1959, it had had the largest floor space of any office building in St. Paul for many years. It became Burlington Northern headquarters in March 1970 but lost that role when Burlington Northern moved its headquarters to Texas in the 1980s.

[ABOVE] Chicago Great Western 156 is leaving the depot at Sargeant with train 5 for Kansas City during the late summer of 1949 or 1950. The mechanical semaphore signals in this photograph display different indications (stop, caution, clear) to the engineer by changing the angle of inclination of the pivoted arm. They were replaced shortly after this image was recorded by color light signals. Collection of Roger W. Bee.

On June 20, 1958, Chicago Great Western train 6 from Kansas City is approaching the crossing with the Rock Island at South St. Paul. This area is nearly unrecognizable in 2012, with the rural scenery of the 1950s replaced by industries and suburban housing. The train in this photograph is unusual since it is only three cars but is being pulled by three diesels; normally only one locomotive handled this train from Kansas City to the Great Northern Station in Minneapolis. Photograph by William D. Middleton.

Waseca was what railroads termed a "division point." In the era of the steam locomotive these were located approximately every one hundred miles. On through trains crews were based and changed out at these points, and there was always a roundhouse for servicing steam locomotives and a yard to sort freight cars. The year 1940 is only twenty-four days away as a Chicago & North Western passenger train pulls away from the Waseca depot on December 7, 1939. Photograph by *Minneapolis Star Journal Tribune,* Minnesota Historical Society Collection.

[ABOVE] The 1940s were busy times for the Duluth-based Duluth, Missabe & Iron Range Railway. Owned by US Steel, it specialized in hauling iron ore from the Mesabi and Vermilion Iron Ranges to the huge docks at Duluth and Two Harbors, where it was transferred to lake boats for movement to blast furnaces along the Great Lakes. Demand for steel increased greatly during World War II and kept up after the war as the economy boomed. In 1942, almost 24 million tons of ore were shipped through the Duluth docks. Duluth, Missabe & Iron Range locomotive 205 is atop Dock 5 in Duluth, where the US Steel steamer *D. M. Clemson* is being loaded. If you look closely you can see workers using poles to move sticky ore out of the dock pockets. Dock 5 was built in 1914 and was last used in 1985. The *D. M. Clemson* was built in 1917 and scrapped in 1980. Photograph from Lake Superior Railroad Museum Collection.

[LEFT] To pull its heavy trains, the Duluth, Missabe & Iron Range employed Mallet locomotives. Mallets were articulated locomotives invented by Swiss engineer Anatole Mallet. They had two engines—two pairs of cylinders, each pair connected by rods to a separate set of driving wheels. The Missabe's 2-8-8-2 Mallets were built in 1916 and rebuilt at the Proctor shops in 1937. They were often used on Proctor Hill, seven miles of heavy grade from the docks in Duluth to the yard in Proctor. In September 1951, Duluth, Missabe & Iron Range 209 is slogging uphill with empty ore cars. The Missabe steam locomotive roster reached an all-time high in 1951, with 172 locomotives. Photograph by Sid Davies; collection of John C. Luecke.

Before the advent of mechanical refrigeration, railroads kept perishables cool using "reefer" cars cooled by ice. Railroads had to maintain large icing facilities where block or crushed ice could be loaded into the cars. It was an expensive, labor-intensive operation. This is the Milwaukee Road's icing facility at Ortonville, on the Minnesota–South Dakota border, in 1949. Ice for the facility was harvested from nearby Big Stone Lake. In the latter half of the twentieth century, mechanical refrigeration began to replace ice-based systems, and mechanical refrigerator units replaced the armies of personnel required to re-ice the cars. Photograph by Peter B. Vikre, Minnesota Historical Society Collection.

The central Minnesota city of Brainerd was the original headquarters of the Northern Pacific Railway, before they moved to St. Paul. The railroad's first shops were also located there, and continued to be Northern Pacific's major locomotive maintenance and rolling stock construction and repair facility on the east end of the system into the 1940s. Hun-dreds of freight cars were built at the Brainerd shops, and the company also built and modified equipment for its own use there. In 1946 shop employees are attaching wood sheathing to cars destined for mainte-nance of way service. Photograph by Powell Krueger, Minnesota Histori-cal Society Collection.

When servicemen returned to civilian life after World War II, many sought employment with the railroads. Several railroad jobs required specialized training, such as telegrapher. To meet the needs of the railroads, the Gale Institute in Minneapolis set up classes to teach telegraphers their trade for service on the nation's railroads. Ronald V. Nixon, a Northern Pacific telegrapher, obtained a second job teaching his trade at the institute. In October 1947 he is standing at left wearing a speakerphone. Photograph by Ronald V. Nixon, Museum of the Rockies Photo Archive.

Steam locomotives were labor-intensive machines. The evidence can be found at Dilworth in the 1940s, where Northern Pacific train 1, the *North Coast Limited,* has stopped for servicing. Four workers can be seen swarming around 4-8-4 No. 2676, checking over various parts of the huge locomotive. The two employees in the center are using an Alemite grease gun to inject grease into 2676's rods, which are connected to the crankpins of the locomotive's driving wheels. No. 2676 will soon be bumped from the plum North Coast Limited assignment—there are new streamlined cars mixed in the train, and the train will go diesel in 1947. This locomotive was the last surviving Northern Pacific 4-8-4-type. It was not scrapped until 1965. Photograph from Lake Superior Railroad Museum Collection.

When the Twin Zephyrs were introduced, the Burlington issued this pamphlet that included a map and a description of the route along the Mississippi, along which the railroad claimed, "Nature Smiles 300 Miles." Author's collection.

In the 1930s there was vigorous competition among the Burlington, Chicago & North Western, and Milwaukee Road for passenger business between Chicago and the Twin Cities. Burlington's trains were the streamlined *Twin Zephyrs,* inaugurated in April 1935 with two three-car trains, but they lacked sufficient capacity. A second pair of six-car trains was ordered as replacements, and these were soon expanded to seven cars. They entered service on December 18, 1936, as the *Morning Zephyr* and the *Afternoon Zephyr.* In 1947, Burlington reequipped the *Twin Zephyrs* with new equipment, including dome cars. They consisted of a baggage-buffet lounge car, four Vista Dome coaches, a diner, and a dome parlor observation car. The stainless steel *Morning Zephyr* is arriving in St. Paul on an afternoon in the 1950s seen from atop a signal bridge. On the right is Northern Pacific's commissary facility; the state capitol is visible in the distance. Collection of John C. Luecke.

[OPPOSITE] From the middle of the nineteenth century until the 1960s, American railroads earned substantial revenues through contracts to carry mail on passenger trains or separate, specialized high-speed mail trains. The trains carried railway post office (RPO) cars, staffed by Railway Mail Service clerks, who sorted, picked up, and dropped off mail en route. In 1948, there were 794 RPO lines operating over 161,000 miles of railroad, but by 1962 only 262 RPO routes were still operating. On March 23, 1949, clerks are sorting mail aboard a Great Northern RPO at the St. Paul Union Depot. In 1967 the U.S. Post Office canceled most rail mail contracts, which had a devastating effect on passenger train revenues. Photograph by *St. Paul Dispatch and Pioneer Press,* Minnesota Historical Society Collection.

[ABOVE] Railroaders love to pose for photographs, particularly with locomotives. Soo Line's management team has gathered at its Shoreham shops in Minneapolis on an October day in 1947 to inspect the railroad's first road diesel, F3 No. 200, fresh from the Electro-Motive factory. While not the Soo's first diesels (switch engines used in yards came first), F3s were its first road freight diesel locomotives, the predecessors of hundreds to follow. The railroad would be dieselized in February 1955 but retained several steam locomotives for possible use between Minneapolis and Sault Ste. Marie, Michigan. Soo Line photograph, Lake Superior Railroad Museum Collection.

[ABOVE] This crew of Soo Liners is posing with 0-6-0 switch engine 344 in Duluth on January 27, 1954. The occasion is unknown, but with steam on the way out, it's possible these railroaders were posing for the last run of a steam locomotive. Photograph from Lake Superior Railroad Museum Collection.

[OPPOSITE, ABOVE] A lesser-known Minnesota-based railroad was the Chicago, St. Paul, Minneapolis & Omaha (Omaha Road). Through most of its existence the Chicago & North Western owned the majority of its stock, but the Omaha maintained a separate identity, with its own office building in St. Paul. On January 1, 1957, it was leased to the North Western and operations were integrated into its parent company. The Omaha's St. Paul shop was along Randolph Street, two miles west of downtown. First opened in 1880, the shop grew and eventually included a fully circular roundhouse with forty stalls. On August 8, 1950, a worker probes the innards of a diesel while other employees concentrate on steam locomotives. Photograph by *St. Paul Dispatch Pioneer Press,* Minnesota Historical Society Collection.

[OPPOSITE, BELOW] Omaha Road 2-8-2 No. 406 is creeping onto the turntable at Randolph Street on January 2, 1955. The diesel era and the Chicago & North Western consolidation spelled doom for the shop—it was closed by the early 1960s—but a portion of the roundhouse remained standing for several decades in nonrail use. Photograph by Wayne C. Olsen; collection of John C. Luecke.

Even though patronage was dropping, Chicago & North Western's *Twin Cities 400* between Minneapolis and Chicago was still a substantial train in the 1950s. The train was prepared for departure at Omaha Road's West Minneapolis coach yard along the Mississippi River north of the Great Northern Station. The 400's engineer signs in for duty [LEFT], then stops to visit with his coworkers in the locker room at the roundhouse adjacent to the coach yard [ABOVE]. The "B.L.F. & E." on the wall stands for "Brotherhood of Locomotive Firemen and Enginemen." He then climbs into the cab of his locomotive [OPPOSITE, TOP] and will take the train from the coach yard to the Great Northern Depot. These three photographs were taken on May 9, 1951. West Minneapolis closed in 1968 and was razed in 1969. Apartments and townhouses now cover the site. *St. Paul Dispatch and Pioneer Press* photographs, Minnesota Historical Society Collection.

[RIGHT] With passengers all aboard, the train makes a rapid departure for St. Paul, seen from the Third Avenue Bridge south of the station. In less than seven hours, the train will arrive at North Western Terminal in Chicago. Collection of John C. Luecke.

[OPPOSITE] While this photograph appears to be in a rural area, it is actually less than a mile from the Minneapolis Great Northern Station. The northernmost terminal on the Chicago Great Western was on Boom Island, just northwest of Nicollet Island along the Mississippi River, acquired from the Wisconsin Central in 1909. In the early 1950s a short passenger train is moving from the Boom Island Yard across a bridge to Nicollet Island, where it will switch to Great Northern Railway tracks into the station. While the Boom Island tracks are gone, both the bridge and pedestrian walkway survive in 2012. Photograph by Al Wallin; collection of John C. Luecke.

[ABOVE] South of downtown Minneapolis is Northern Pacific Bridge 9 over the Mississippi River. Constructed in 1887, the bridge was part of a major relocation project to remove Northern Pacific's tracks from the University of Minnesota campus. In 1922 a contract was executed with the university to abandon the line, relocating it adjacent to the Great Northern Railway north of the campus. This required moving the Northern Pacific bridge about one thousand feet upstream. The railroad reused some of the trusses from the old bridge, and the new bridge was completed in 1923. In September 1955, two steam locomotives are crossing the bridge with a special for Stillwater for the dedication of displayed Northern Pacific steam locomotive 328. This bridge is now a hiking and biking trail. Photograph from Ronald V. Nixon Collection, Museum of the Rockies Photo Archive.

On November 10, 1958, Chicago & North Western (Omaha Road) train 203, the *North American* to Omaha, is crossing Mississippi River Bridge 15, just west of downtown St. Paul. Above the locomotive is the Schmidt Brewery. Bridge 15 is a swing bridge constructed by the Chicago, St. Paul, Minneapolis & Omaha and the Chicago, Milwaukee & St. Paul (Milwaukee Road) in 1915. It is still in use today by Canadian Pacific and Union Pacific. *The North American* wasn't so lucky—it was discontinued in November 1959. Photograph by William D. Middleton.

West of Bridge 15 in St. Paul was the Omaha Road's Western Avenue Yard and Milwaukee Road's busy Short Line, which got its name in 1880 when it was constructed as a shortcut for the Milwaukee Road between Minneapolis and St. Paul. Dropping down Short Line Hill on March 22, 1958, is Rock Island's *Twin Star Rocket,* heading from Minneapolis to Houston, Texas. Below the train is Western Avenue Yard, while Bridge 15 is just out of sight behind the power plant. Above the *Rocket*'s third car is Ancker Hospital, which was demolished in 1967. Photograph by William D. Middleton.

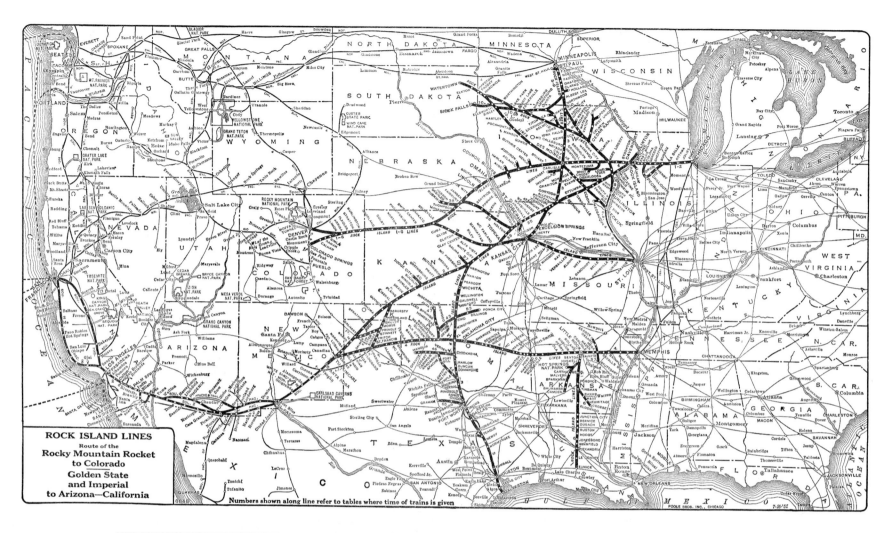

ROCK ISLAND LINES
Route of the
Rocky Mountain Rocket
to Colorado
Golden State
and Imperial
to Arizona—California

Numbers shown along line refer to tables where time of trains is given

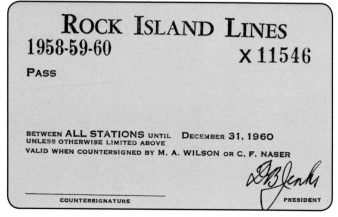

ROCK ISLAND LINES
1958-59-60
X 11546

PASS

BETWEEN ALL STATIONS UNTIL   DECEMBER 31, 1960
UNLESS OTHERWISE LIMITED ABOVE
VALID WHEN COUNTERSIGNED BY M. A. WILSON OR C. F. NASER

_____
COUNTERSIGNATURE   PRESIDENT

[ABOVE] While thought of mainly as a Midwest railroad, the Rock Island served the South as well, with lines reaching from Minneapolis to Texas, Louisiana, and New Mexico, as seen in this timetable map. Author's collection.

[LEFT] Passes for travel on passenger trains were mainly given out to railroad executives, employees, family members, and special guests. They were usually printed on thick, colored card stock paper and featured the name of the holder, the date of issue, and the name of the railroad. This is a Rock Island pass from 1958 to 1960 and signed by Downing B. Jenks, the railroad's president. Author's collection.

[ABOVE] Soo Line passenger trains arriving in Minneapolis from the west followed a complex route to reach the Milwaukee Road Depot. They followed the west bank of the Mississippi to the Great Northern Station, went though a short tunnel on the station's west side, passed by the Minneapolis Post Office, ducked under Third Avenue and First Street South, and emerged at the throat tracks of the Milwaukee Road Depot. This is Soo Line train 14, the combined *Winnipeger* and *Soo-Dominion*, passing under the First Street South Bridge to enter the tracks leading to the Milwaukee Road Depot on May 4, 1958. After moving ahead about another city block, the train will back into the station. The factory building in the background is now home to the University of Minnesota Press. Photograph by William D. Middleton.

[RIGHT] A few minutes later Soo Line 504, which had brought the train into the depot, stands to the side as another Soo Line diesel switches the train. In the center is Milwaukee Road's *Olympian Hiawatha* from Seattle/Tacoma, which will soon depart for Chicago. To the left are the diesels that brought in the overnight *Pioneer Limited* from Chicago. Above them can be seen the Metropolitan Building. Constructed in 1890, it is considered Minneapolis's first skyscraper and one of the most architecturally significant structures in the city. It was demolished in 1961 as part of urban renewal efforts. Its destruction provided a catalyst for historic preservation movements in Minneapolis and across Minnesota. Photograph by William D. Middleton.

[ABOVE] Soo Line and Rock Island trains congregate under the train shed at the Milwaukee Road Depot along Washington Avenue. On the left is Soo Line train 62 for Duluth with 4-6-2 No. 727 in the lead, while on the right is one of Rock Island's Rocket trains about to depart for Des Moines and Kansas City. Photograph by John W. Malven; collection of Stuart J. Nelson.

[RIGHT] The Milwaukee Road's *Olympian* and *Twin Cities Hiawatha*, which served the Milwaukee Road Depot, were the first streamliners to feature full-length dome cars. The new cars entered service in 1952, and the Milwaukee advertised them extensively. This ad in *National Geographic* boasted of the scenic views from the dome on the *Olympian Hiawatha*. Author's collection.

The evening of August 28, 1958, finds the *Soo-Dominion* for Vancouver, British Columbia, nosed up to the bumper posts just outside the waiting room of the Milwaukee Road Depot. Because it was a stub-end station and Soo Line trains ran through, their trains from St. Paul would run locomotive first into the depot and then back out to depart. Trains from the west backed in and left for St. Paul engine first. The large chutes above the locomotive were openings that allowed steam locomotive smoke to escape through the roof of the train shed. They were preserved when the depot was restored in the 1990s. Photograph by William D. Middleton.

Soaring above the Mississippi River, the Rock Island's *Twin Star Rocket* crosses the Short Line Bridge en route from Minneapolis to Houston on February 16, 1958. The 1,144-foot double-track bridge, a familiar sight to generations of Minneapolitans, was constructed in 1880. It was built by the Milwaukee Road as part of a project to shorten the line between Minneapolis and St. Paul, which at the time took a roundabout route through Mendota. Now single track, the bridge is used only by terminal railroad Minnesota Commercial to reach several customers along Hiawatha Avenue in Minneapolis. Photograph by William D. Middleton.

Between 1912 and 1917, the Milwaukee Road constructed the Twenty-Ninth Street grade relocation in Minneapolis. The project involved lowering the tracks approximately twenty feet on a three-mile stretch between Cedar and Hennepin Avenues, parallel to Twenty-Ninth Street and Lake Street. The line had nearly forty street crossings that were replaced with thirty-seven reinforced concrete bridges—so many that the line resembled a long tunnel. In the early 1950s a Milwaukee Road train is approaching one of the few remaining grade crossings, which has flooded and is being guarded by flagmen while children use the water to cool off. Today this is the Midtown Greenway rail trail. Photograph by Emil Skok; collection of John C. Luecke.

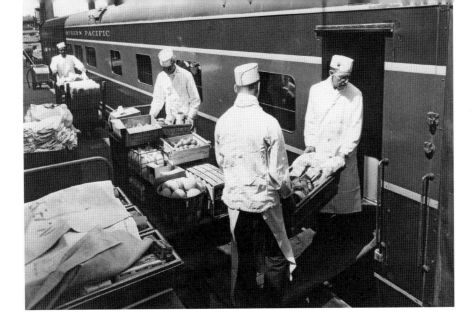

[ABOVE] "Famously good food" was how Northern Pacific advertised its dining car meals. That food was loaded aboard Northern Pacific diners at the commissary at the Third Street coach yard in St. Paul, just east of the Union Depot. In August 1952, dining car department employees are stocking a streamlined diner for Northern Pacific's flagship train, the *North Coast Limited,* which operated between Chicago, Minneapolis/ St. Paul, Seattle, and Portland. Each railroad typically maintained commissaries at key points on its system to keep their dining cars fully stocked. Minnesota Historical Society Collection.

[OPPOSITE] One of the longest running traditions on the Northern Pacific was the production of Christmas fruitcakes. The railroad's recipe earned an international grand prize at the London Caterer's Exposition in 1873. Starting in 1910, the bakery at the St. Paul commissary produced thousands of cakes every Christmas season, not only for its dining cars but also for sale to the public, except during times of war. In 1955, Northern Pacific master baker J. F. Welligrant is removing pans of fruitcake from the oven at the commissary. The tradition of producing fruitcakes ended in 1967. Photograph by Northern Pacific Railway, Minnesota Historical Society Collection.

[RIGHT] The steward in the dining car of the *North Coast Limited* catches up on some paperwork as the train races through the night between St. Paul and Fargo in 1959. Dining car stewards were responsible for supervising the activities of the workers who prepared, cooked, and delivered food to passengers; ordering food and supplies, such as linen, cookware, and silverware; and seating passengers and collecting payment from customers. Stewards also maintained records of all cash received. Photograph by William D. Middleton.

[ABOVE] The year 1955 was the 150th anniversary of the Lewis and Clark expedition. To commemorate the event, Northern Pacific's Como Shops in St. Paul rebuilt six 1947 lounge cars into "Lewis & Clark Traveller's Rest" lounge cars for the *North Coast Limited*. The cars featured large murals painted by Chicago artist Edgar Miller with scenes taken from the journals of Lewis and Clark. Included was a map showing the explorers' route, scenes from a buffalo hunt, and paintings of Indians and wild animals. The murals were hand-painted, so each car was slightly different. In this publicity photograph, passengers are enjoying the lounge section of the car with the mural on the ceiling above. Notice the weedy track outside, which indicates that this photograph was probably staged in a yard or at Como Shops. Photograph by Northern Pacific Railway, Minnesota Historical Society Collection.

[OPPOSITE] One of the Lewis & Clark Traveller's Rest cars is being repaired at Como Shops in St. Paul on April 19, 1959. Photograph by William D. Middleton.

[ABOVE] When a loaded Duluth, Missabe & Iron Range ore train arrived at Alborn from the Mesabi Range, the steam locomotive would uncouple from its train and move across the highway crossing to take on water at a water plug. After filling the tender, the engine would back up, couple onto the train, and whistle in the flagman. The flagman would be protecting the rear of the train, and after hearing the whistle he would climb back in the caboose. The train would then start south in a volcanic eruption of smoke and steam, as Yellowstone 226 demonstrates leaving Alborn for Proctor in September 1955. Photograph by James Kreuzberger, Minnesota Streetcar Museum Collection.

[OPPOSITE, ABOVE] Duluth, Missabe & Iron Range's eighteen Yellowstone-class locomotives, built in 1941 and 1943, were among the world's most powerful steam locomotives. The railroad was justifiably proud of the machines and publicized them extensively, even after the railroad dieselized. Yellowstone 227 is passing the well-kept depot at Allen Junction near Hoyt Lakes, heading south with a trainload of iron ore from the Vermilion Iron Range for the docks at Two Harbors. This view was taken from a coaling tower. No. 227 was preserved and is displayed at the Lake Superior Railroad Museum in Duluth. Lake Superior Railroad Museum Collection.

[OPPOSITE, MIDDLE] To maintain their cars and locomotives, railroads built huge shop complexes. Brainerd, Minneapolis, Proctor, St. Cloud, St. Paul, and Two Harbors had large shops. Duluth, Missabe & Iron Range Railway's Two Harbors shops were responsible for overhauls on the Missabe's Yellowstone locomotives such as 227 at the shop in 1952. With the arrival of diesels, Duluth, Missabe & Iron Range planned new diesel shops for both Proctor and Two Harbors. When the Proctor shop opened it was able to handle all diesel work. Plans for a second diesel facility at Two Harbors were shelved, and when the steam shops were closed, Two Harbors was no longer a shop town. Photograph by James Kreuenberger, Minnesota Streetcar Museum Collection.

[OPPOSITE, BELOW] This is the view the fireman had down the long boiler of a Yellowstone as it arrived in Proctor in the 1950s. That boiler provided plenty of protection for the crew if there was a collision at a grade crossing. Collection of John C. Luecke.

[FAR RIGHT] Duluth, Missabe & Iron Range's huge yard and shop facility at Proctor, seven miles from Duluth, is seen from the top of the yard's coaling dock. The nearly circular Proctor roundhouse is on the right, and the new diesel shop is to the left. Stored steam locomotives, most never to run again, are in the foreground, while their new diesel replacements idle outside the shop. The steam era on the Missabe Road is rapidly drawing to a close. Collection of John C. Luecke.

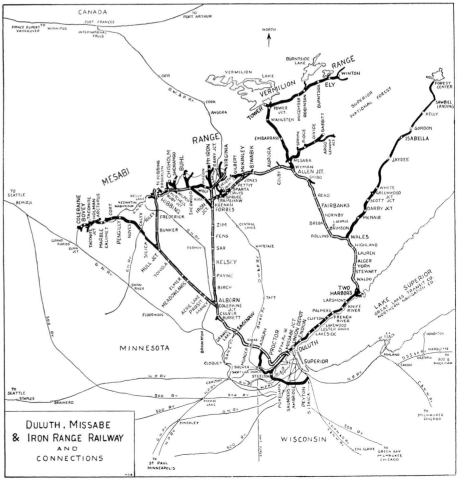

[RIGHT, BELOW] The Duluth, Missabe & Iron Range Railway serviced both the Mesabi and Vermilion Iron Ranges once served by its predecessors, the Duluth, Missabe & Northern and the Duluth & Iron Range. The two roads merged in 1938. Author's collection.

DULUTH, MISSABE
& IRON RANGE RAILWAY
AND
CONNECTIONS

Railroading is a twenty-four-hour business, which means operating personnel—engineers, conductors, yard workers, and many others—must work at night. During the steam era many thought of railroading as a glamorous occupation, but it could also be a difficult one, particularly during the night hours as crews fought sleep to get their trains over the road. Duluth, Missabe & Iron Range engineer Ed App is at the throttle of Yellowstone 228 as it heads south for Proctor with a train of ore loads on the night of May 26, 1959. Photograph by William D. Middleton.

Later that night App brings his big locomotive up to the scale track at Proctor so the train can be weighed. US Steel, the railroad's owner, wanted to know how much ore was actually making it to the ports for tax, billing, and royalty reasons, so the Missabe installed scales at Proctor and north of Two Harbors to weigh cars. This train consisted of 190 loaded cars with a gross weight of 17,468 tons. Photograph by William D. Middleton.

At the beginning and end of the shipping season, with cold weather early in the spring and late in the fall, Duluth, Missabe & Iron Range was forced to thaw carloads of iron ore. Moisture in the cars would freeze, making dumping impossible. The railroad ran underground steam pipes to portions of its yards in Proctor and Two Harbors, which carried steam from locomotives to special pipes that could be inserted into ore cars for thawing. The cars were then rushed to the docks for dumping. Locomotives used in the operation produced huge clouds of smoke and steam over the yards, such as at Two Harbors in the 1950s. Lake Superior Railroad Museum Collection.

Diesel locomotive builders took their locomotives on the road to con-vince railroads to purchase their products. In July 1955, Electro-Motive sent its 1,750-horsepower SD9 demonstrator 5591 to the Duluth, Missa-be & Iron Range, which was still largely steam powered. The Missabe Road used it for several months, resulting in an order for ten SD9s for 1956 delivery. Three more orders for SD9s followed. No. 5591 is pulling a local train at Iron Junction in September 1955. It stayed on as part of the 1956 order and was numbered 110. Photograph by James Kreuzberger, Minnesota Streetcar Museum Collection.

Near the end of steam operations on the Duluth, Winnipeg & Pacific, 2-8-0 No. 2457 approaches the coaling tower at the railroad's West Duluth Yard on March 30, 1956. Steam power on the Duluth, Winnipeg & Pacific reflected the influence of its parent, Canadian National. The number boards and cab and tender lettering all followed the Canadian National style. The coaling tower on the right was installed at West Duluth in 1949, but it had a short life—the last steam operation on the railroad was Duluth–Fort Frances passenger train 19 on April 6, 1957. Freight operations fell to diesels in 1956. Photograph by William D. Middleton.

Reserve Mining Company constructed an entirely new, forty-seven-mile railroad between Babbitt and Silver Bay from 1953 to 1955. To bring in supplies, Reserve Mining relied on a new connection with the Duluth, Missabe & Iron Range at a location called Norshor Junction, approximately twenty-five miles north of Two Harbors. In January 1952, six-month-old Reserve Mining switch engines 650 and 651 are moving around the small yard at the junction, where new railroad ties and other supplies are being unloaded. After Reserve Mining's railroad was completed, it began moving trains of raw taconite ore from the mining area at Babbitt to the processing plant at Silver Bay, on the north shore of Lake Superior. Photograph by James Kreuzberger, Minnesota Streetcar Museum Collection.

[ABOVE] In July 1961, an Erie Mining taconite train drops downgrade into Taconite Harbor with loads from Hoyt Lakes. When Erie Mining's F9 diesels arrived in 1956, they were painted in the blue and silver colors seen here. In the 1960s Erie Mining switched to yellow and maroon paint. Color photographs of the original paint scheme are quite rare, since few took the time to visit the isolated railroad in the 1950s and 1960s. Collection of Aaron Isaacs.

[RIGHT] In 1957 Erie Mining Company opened its seventy-two-mile private railroad to haul taconite pellets between Hoyt Lakes and Taconite Harbor. Erie's line was remote and rugged, traversing an area with few roads and requiring a considerable amount of cutting and filling to build through the rough terrain. Railroaders love to inspect their properties, so Erie Mining ran this special to look over the new railroad in 1957. It stopped on the remote Manitou River Bridge with new F9A 104 pulling Erie Mining's private car Taconite Trail. The car was built in 1927 as the Sunbeam and was purchased from the Pullman Company in 1956. Photograph by Erie Mining Company; collection of Doug Buell.

Minnesota was once home to a large number of electric railways that served cities such as the Twin Cities, Duluth, Brainerd, and Winona. The last electric railway to operate was the Mesaba-Cliffs Mining Company line at Marble. Owned by Cleveland-Cliffs Iron Company, it operated from a loading area at the Hill-Trumbull mine at Marble to a concentrator plant near Calumet, a distance of about one and three-quarter miles. Trains normally consisted of five to seven cars carrying iron ore. Missaba-Cliffs 206 is pushing a loaded train to the concentrator as it crosses Highway 169 and goes under the Great Northern Railway near Marble in September 1955. No. 206 and two other electrics, 204 and 205, were used until the end of operations in 1972. Photograph by James Kreuzberger, Minnesota Streetcar Museum Collection.

[ABOVE] Soo Line's elegant passenger depot in Duluth opened for business on October 3, 1910. In 1951 the Soo inaugurated a new Duluth–Chicago train, the *Laker*, and the depot received upgraded ticket windows, seen in this March 1952 publicity photograph. Lake Superior Railroad Museum Collection.

[LEFT] Down on track level, the *Laker* gets a once-over prior to its evening departure. Even though the Soo rebuilt and updated cars for the train and assigned diesels to pull it, ridership on the *Laker* declined in the late 1950s. To save money, Soo moved the train's northern terminus from Duluth to Superior, Wisconsin, on May 20, 1961. Lake Superior Railroad Museum Collection.

On August 18, 1958, Soo train 65, the local for Thief River Falls, departs the elegant station and is about to roll into the 1,631-foot tunnel under Michigan Street, completed in 1909. The last regular passenger trains to use the depot were trains 62 and 63 between Duluth and St. Paul on June 25, 1961. The building was demolished in August 1972. Photograph by William D. Middleton.

[ABOVE] On February 6, 1955, the Minnesota Railfans Association ran an excursion with new Northern Pacific rail diesel cars. Just north of White Bear Lake was Bald Eagle, where the Northern Pacific line to Duluth crossed Soo Line's route to Duluth and Sault Ste. Marie. Fans unloaded to photograph their train, but got a double treat as a steam-powered Soo ski special showed up heading for Dresser, Wisconsin. Powered by 4007, it was the last run of a Soo Line 4-8-2 steam locomotive. This photograph shows the long-vanished interlocking tower and Bald Eagle depot. Two railroads—Canadian Pacific and Minnesota Commercial—still cross here in 2012. Photograph by John W. Malven; collection of Stuart J. Nelson.

[OPPOSITE, ABOVE] Forming a perfect silhouette against the winter sun, Soo Line St. Paul–Enderlin, North Dakota, local train 5 crosses the Crow River at Rockford in the waning days of steam in the early 1950s. Photograph by John W. Malven; collection of Stuart J. Nelson.

[OPPOSITE, BELOW] In March 1954, train 5 pulls into Paynesville as the depot operator hands up orders to the fireman of engine 2717. The Griswold Signal Company of Minneapolis, founded by Minnesota native Frank W. Griswold, manufactured the crossing signal in the foreground. They were once common in the Midwest and featured a combination of highway flasher and rotating stop sign. An approaching train triggered the red flashing lights and bells as well as a mechanism that rotated a yellow stop sign, such as the one seen here, ninety degrees to face roadway traffic. Photograph by James Kreuzberger, Minnesota Streetcar Museum Collection.

[ABOVE] The clickity-clack sound of wheels hitting rail joints lulled many a passenger to sleep over the years, but in the mid-twentieth century railroads began to move away from jointed rail to continuous welded rail. Because there are few joints, this form of track is very strong, gives a smoother ride, and needs less maintenance; trains can travel at higher speeds and with less friction. Welded rail is more expensive to lay than jointed, but it has much lower maintenance costs. A Soo Line crew lays down welded rail just east of the depot at Moose Lake in July 1956. Collection of Stuart J. Nelson.

[LEFT, TOP] The Soo Line constructed two-story depots in several towns, which it referred to as "second-class" depots. There were a number of variations: some were built longer with more baggage room area; some had the baggage room on one end, and others had it on the opposite end. Waiting rooms also varied in style. The two-story depots all had one thing in common: living quarters above the depot for the agent and operator. Some living areas had three bedrooms, but most had only two. The local for Thief River Falls is passing the well-maintained second-class depot at Newfolden in August 1957. Photograph by Stuart J. Nelson.

[LEFT, MIDDLE] Another second-class depot stood at Remer, where train 64 is stopping on June 23, 1956. Local passenger trains like this were the lifeblood of many communities. As roads improved and highways were built, many of these trains survived on mail contracts, and when those disappeared, so did the trains. Locals 64 and 65 provided railway post office, less-than-carload freight, and passenger service over the Plummer Line from Duluth to Thief River Falls with a combination car that handled all three functions. Even with this economy, the train couldn't survive, and the last runs were made on May 16, 1959. Photograph by Stuart J. Nelson.

If you purchased your ticket from the conductor on board a train instead of at a station, you received a receipt such as this one issued by the Soo Line for 76 cents. Author's collection.

Soo Line also had "first-class" depots, with one story, that usually included a waiting room, office for the depot agent, and a baggage room. The agent-operator sold tickets, communicated with the dispatcher by phone or telegraph, kept track of cars in town, and communicated with the public. On July 12, 1958, the Moose Lake agent is about to hand up orders to the caboose of an empty ore train heading to the Cuyuna Iron Range. The Moose Lake Area Historical Society has preserved the depot. Photograph by William D. Middleton.

[OPPOSITE] Inside Soo Line's Shoreham shops in Minneapolis in August 1958, a welder is at work on locomotive 207-B, an American Locomotive model FA road diesel. Workers at railroad shops were well paid, thanks to the strength of railroad unions and the fact that special training and skills were required to work on locomotives and cars. Working for the railroad also meant job security, since railroads were profitable enterprises, at least into the 1960s. Today most railroads contract out their major locomotive overhauls, although a handful of shops remain in operation. Photograph by William D. Middleton.

[ABOVE] Steam power is in its last years as Great Northern 2-8-2 No. 3117 works a local at milepost 23 near Richmond on the line between Willmar and St. Cloud in September 1955. In 1955 Great Northern operated 1,289,743 train miles with steam power. By 1957, the last year in which steam power operated before dieselization, Great Northern steam locomotives ran only 10,034 freight train miles. No. 3117, built in 1918, was retired in 1957 but not scrapped until 1962. Photograph by James Kreuzberger, Minnesota Streetcar Museum Collection.

[RIGHT] Pounding west on the double-track Great Northern Railway main line, Great Northern 2-8-2 No. 3363 is passing the Minneapolis & St. Louis's Cedar Lake Yard on the western outskirts of downtown Minneapolis. It's an eighty-eight-mile trip from here to the division point at Willmar. Collection of John C. Luecke.

One way that railroads saved money on branch line passenger service was by operating mixed trains, which hauled both freight and passenger cars. Great Northern ran a mixed train, which originated in Minneapolis, on the forty-four-mile Hutchinson Branch from Wayzata to Hutchinson. From the 1950s into the 1970s, a rare General Motors NW5 locomotive powered the local train on the branch—only thirteen were ever constructed. Its proximity to the Twin Cities made it a popular train with rail enthusiasts. On February 17, 1958, NW5 186 leads the mixed train west near Mound. This branch was abandoned in 2001. Photograph by William D. Middleton.

Paralleling the Hutchinson Branch just to the north was the Luce Line, named after the Luce family, who owned most of the stock of predecessor Electric Short Line Railway Company. When incorporated in 1908, backers of this railroad hoped to build a line between Minneapolis and Watertown, South Dakota. The portion from Minneapolis to Hutchinson was completed in 1915 and to Lake Lillian in 1923, but the railroad fell into foreclosure in 1924. Control shifted to the Minnesota Western Railroad, incorporated by the railroad's bondholders and operated by the Minneapolis, Northfield & Southern Railway beginning in 1927, the year an extension to the tiny town of Gluek was finished, which turned out to be the end of the line. In 1956 the Minneapolis & St. Louis acquired the Minnesota Western and changed its name to the Minneapolis Industrial Railway in 1959. Rarely photographed, the lonely line hosted an excursion train from Minneapolis to Hutchinson on March 16, 1958, seen during a stop at Watertown. Operations between Hutchinson and Gluek were suspended in 1967, and the 104 miles from Plymouth to Gluek were abandoned in 1972. The Luce Line State Trail was constructed over much of the right-of-way. Photograph by William D. Middleton.

[LEFT, ABOVE] Always a pro-passenger railroad, Great Northern operated a fleet of secondary trains on its Minnesota routes in addition to its transcontinental streamliners. Among the best was the *Red River,* introduced in 1950 on the Grand Forks, North Dakota–St. Paul route. The mini-streamliner departed Grand Forks in the morning and arrived at St. Paul Union Depot in midafternoon. It was then turned and serviced for an early evening departure for Grand Forks. On April 13, 1958, the eastbound *Red River* is passing Great Northern's Mississippi Street coach yard and the tower at Jackson Street on its last lap into the St. Paul Union Depot. Retired Great Northern employee Gary Nelson recalled that as the eastbound *Empire Builder* and *Western Star* passed the coach yard, employees inspected the trains, looking for defects that would be repaired when the trains were brought into the yard. Today the bridge above the tracks at this location carries Interstate Highway 35E. Photograph by William D. Middleton.

[LEFT, BELOW] Just west of the Mississippi Street coach yard was Great Northern's Jackson Street shop complex. The roundhouse and diesel shop maintained locomotives, and another part of the complex was devoted to passenger car maintenance and repair. To move cars between buildings, a transfer table was used. Similar in function to a turntable (though it cannot be used to turn equipment around) a transfer table saves space and serves multiple stalls. A transfer table is a short length of track on a platform; the platform is be moved sideways along tracks perpendicular to the transfer table, positioning the engine or car in front of the appropriate stall. In March 1962 observation car *Cathedral Mountain* is taking a ride on the transfer table at Jackson Street. Photograph by Byron D. Olsen.

[OPPOSITE] When the *Red River* began service on June 25, 1950, it included an observation-diner-lounge car, also named *Red River*. Full dining service was offered in a twelve-seat dinette area of the car, while light snacks were available in the adjoining nine-seat coffee shop. The tapered parlor and observation section included seating in chairs and a settee. This photograph was taken by the railway to show off the amenities of the car prior to the streamliner entering service. It was rebuilt into a coach in 1963. Photograph by *Minneapolis Star Tribune,* Minnesota Historical Society Collection.

The photographer has climbed atop the coaling dock at Northern Pacific's Northtown Yard in Minneapolis, giving us a bird's-eye view of the locomotive and car shops at the yard. Steam locomotives are still in evidence, along with new diesels. The roundhouse and turntable are straight ahead; behind them is the Soo Line main line out of Shoreham Yard. To the right is the car repair facility. These buildings were demolished when Burlington Northern remodeled Northtown after the 1970 merger, but the turntable was salvaged and installed just north of a new diesel shop Burlington Northern constructed. Collection of John C. Luecke.

Looking from inside the cab of a Northern Pacific F3 diesel at Northtown, the coaling dock is visible, along with a portion of the roundhouse and GP9 No. 286, flying white flags that indicate its last move was as an extra, which was not in the timetable. Collection of John C. Luecke.

[OPPOSITE, ABOVE] Until the 1950s U.S. presidents and candidates traveled primarily by rail. Beginning in 1942, President Roosevelt and his successors traveled in a specially modified private car, the *Ferdinand Magellan*. The car was armor-plated with five-eighths-inch-thick steel on the roof, floor, and sides and was fitted with three-inch-thick windows and two escape hatches. It weighed 285,000 pounds. When the president traveled, his special train moved under the code name POTUS (President of the United States). POTUS specials occasionally came to Minnesota, exemplified by President Harry S. Truman waving from the rear of the *Ferdinand Magellan* in Minneapolis on November 3, 1949. Minnesota Historical Society Collection.

[OPPOSITE, BELOW] Truman's successor, Dwight D. Eisenhower, shakes hands with supporters during the 1952 campaign outside the Milwaukee Road depot in Northfield. Eisenhower was the last president to use the special car, switching to air travel during his term. Photograph by Philip C. Dittes, Minnesota Historical Society Collection.

[ABOVE] Between Northern Pacific's Northtown Yard in Minneapolis and St. Cloud, Great Northern and Northern Pacific jointly operated a double-track main line. One track was owned by Great Northern, the other by Northern Pacific. This busy stretch of track paralleled U.S. Highway 10 for much of the distance, allowing for scenes such as Northern Pacific 4-8-4 No. 2677 speeding west with a freight train, photographed from a car on the paralleling highway west of Anoka. The weather must be warm as the fireman has the windows slid open in the all-weather vestibule cab of the 2677. Photograph by John Malven; collection of John C. Luecke.

[RIGHT] On another day on the joint Great Northern–Northern Pacific double track, a Northern Pacific freight steams west under a cloud of smoke as the caboose of an eastbound recedes in the distance. Photograph by John Malven; collection of John C. Luecke.

[BELOW] With losses from passenger train operations mounting in the 1950s, some railroads turned to rail diesel cars to save money. These self-propelled passenger cars provided cost savings over traditional steam-powered trains on lesser-traveled routes. In the 1950s and 1960s, Canadian National; Duluth, Missabe & Iron Range; Duluth, Winnipeg & Pacific; Northern Pacific; and Minneapolis & St. Louis experimented with rail diesel cars on runs in the state. Beginning in 1953 Duluth, Missabe & Iron Range's single car made a daily round-trip between Duluth and Ely and Winton. The car is at the Winton depot in July 1957. The children are taking a ride to Ely to watch a movie and will return home by automobile. Photograph by *Minneapolis Star Tribune,* Minnesota Historical Society Collection.

[RIGHT] Duluth, Missabe & Iron Range RDC 1 was equipped with a railway post office and express section in addition to coach seating. At Winton in July 1957, postmistress Mayme Gustason hands up a pouch of mail to the railway post office clerk. The car made its last run on July 15, 1961, and was sold to the Northern Pacific in 1963. Photograph by *Minneapolis Star Tribune,* Minnesota Historical Society Collection.

[LEFT] Beginning in April 1957, the Duluth, Winnipeg & Pacific offered rail diesel car service between Duluth and Fort Frances, Ontario. Operating on an overnight schedule, the car left Duluth in the evening as train 619 and returned the next morning as train 620. It is dropping down the steep grade into West Duluth on August 1, 1959. Photograph by William D. Middleton.

[OPPOSITE, TOP] The cold night of January 1, 1959, at the Omaha Road's Duluth depot finds Chicago & North Western's train 510, the *Chicago Limited,* and Duluth, Winnipeg & Pacific's rail diesel car preparing for their departures to Chicago and Fort Frances, Ontario, respectively. The steam is coming from boilers in the Chicago & North Western locomotive that heat the train. The sister train of the *Chicago Limited* was the *Duluth–Superior Limited* from Chicago. Photograph by William D. Middleton.

[BELOW] In 1958, Minnesota celebrated its one hundredth birthday, and railroads played a role. Minnesota railroads operated the *Minnesota Centennial Train* filled with documents, artifacts, and displays relating to Minnesota's one hundred years of statehood. Several railroads moved the train across the state. The *Centennial Train* is heading east out of Minneapolis for St. Paul, crossing the famous Stone Arch Bridge over the Mississippi River with a Burlington Route E5 on the head end. The Stone Arch Bridge was owned by Great Northern; Burlington had operating rights over Great Northern track from Minneapolis to St. Paul. Minnesota Historical Society Collection.

When Chicago & North Western added streamlined sleeping cars to its two North Country overnight trains, the Chicago to Duluth *Duluth–Superior Limited* and the Chicago to Twin Cities *North Western Limited,* it issued this brochure, which boasted, "You'll find nothing lacking to mar the enjoyment and restfulness of your trip." Author's collection.

[OPPOSITE, FAR LEFT] As the retirement of steam locomotives accelerated in the 1950s, railroad fans organized excursions to pay their last respects to steam. The Minnesota Railfans Association sponsored dozens of such trips in the 1950s and 1960s, including this one: a round-trip steam excursion on the Northern Pacific from Minneapolis to Staples on June 30, 1957. It featured Northern Pacific 2686, a modern 4-8-4 built by Baldwin in June 1943, seen roaring through a cut at Lincoln, Minnesota, during a run-by for photographers. No. 2686 received three new welded boiler courses in 1952 to extend its service life, but diesels won out and it was dismantled at the Brainerd shops in January 1959. Photograph by Al Wallin; collection of John C. Luecke.

[OPPOSITE, ABOVE] A view east reveals the two-story Staples depot, which housed the railroad offices, ticket windows, and waiting room. A tower just east of the depot guards the junction of the main line to Minneapolis and the route to Duluth–Superior. In 2012 these facilities are gone except for the depot. Freight trains, which used to stop at Staples to change crews, now run through to Dilworth or Minneapolis. The depot is still a stop for Amtrak's *Empire Builder*. Photograph by Perry Becker.

[OPPOSITE, BELOW] Earlier that day, as 2686 was being serviced, Perry Becker climbed to the top of the coaling trestle to capture these panoramic views of the Staples facilities at the end of the steam era. Looking west, the double-track main line to Dilworth and Fargo can be seen, as can the freight house and yard. Winches and cables were used to move gondolas of coal up the steep grade to the top of the dock. Photograph by Perry Becker.

[RIGHT] Northern Pacific scrapped hundreds of steam locomotives at its Brainerd shops. Some were stored at the yard in nearby Staples before making their last trip for dismantling. Included were several of Northern Pacific's Challenger-class 4-6-6-4 locomotives. These modern, powerful machines had a shortened service life because of dieselization. The photographer is standing on the tender of Challenger 5149, the last road steam locomotive purchased by Northern Pacific. Built by American Locomotive in September 1944, it was in service for less than fifteen years and was cut up at Brainerd in September 1959. This photograph reveals the rugged condition of these once-magnificent machines as they await scrapping, including engine 5106, built in 1936. The Challengers were the epitome of steam locomotive design on the Northern Pacific. They burned inexpensive coal, could pull long trains over the mountains and make good time in the valleys and flatlands, and during World War II handled long troop trains. Despite their excellent performance, they were still swept away in the tide of dieselization. Photograph by Perry Becker.

[LEFT] As railroads expanded in the nineteenth century, they were forced to cross one another at grade. To control the crossings, railroads installed interlocker towers. An interlocking is an arrangement of signal apparatus that prevents conflicting movements through tracks at locations such as junctions or crossings. Interlockings were designed so that it was impossible to give clear signals to trains unless the route to be used is safe. An operator lined the route as a train approached, while other routes in the interlocking received a stop signal. Technology eventually caught up with the towers and they were automated, controlled by facilities sometimes hundreds of miles away. The last manned tower in Minnesota was Winona's Tower CK, closed in 1989. Minnesota Transfer owned this tower at the Northern Pacific crossing at Park Junction in Minneapolis, where a Northern Pacific local is coming to a stop for some switching work. This tower was preserved in Heritage Square at the Minnesota State Fairgrounds. Photograph by Emil Skok; collection of John C. Luecke.

[ABOVE, LEFT] In the 1950s railroads were anxious to project a modern, forward-thinking image and were happy to scrap their steam locomotives. One exception was the Burlington Route, whose president, Harry C. Murphy, loved steam locomotives. One of the few railroad executives to recognize the public relations value of steam engines, Murphy kept two operational and set them to work representing the company on special runs well into the 1960s. The larger of the two engines, 4-8-4 No. 5632, is on track 11 at the St. Paul Union Depot ready to head east with an excursion in 1959. The engineer and officials have gathered at the head end to confer before departure. Photograph by Emil Skok; collection of John C. Luecke.

[ABOVE, RIGHT] Towers had large levers that were moved manually by operators to control the interlocking plant. Wires or rods, connected at one end to the signals and tracks and at the other to levers in the tower, ran alongside the tracks. Inside each tower were a track board, which showed the layout of the interlocking, and track manipulation charts, which gave the proper lever arrangements to line up a route. These were helpful for personnel who were not used to a tower. Most operators who had worked at a tower for some time knew the lever arrangements by heart. This is the manipulation chart for the Hoffman Avenue Tower just east of downtown St. Paul in 1972. This concrete tower fell to the wrecker's ball at 10:25 a.m. on April 17, 1986. Photograph by William Cordes, Minnesota Streetcar Museum Collection.

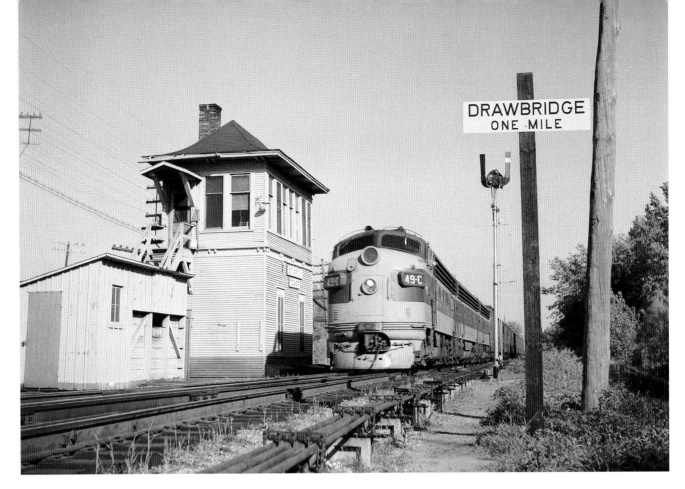

[ABOVE] In Hastings, St. Croix Tower controlled the junction between the busy Burlington Route and Milwaukee Road main lines from Chicago. From St. Croix Tower to St. Paul, the two railroads operated the track jointly, with either railroad using the two main tracks, which were controlled by a dispatcher at a tower in Newport. On May 19, 1958, Milwaukee Road freight 63 is passing the tower. The rear of the train is still on the drawbridge over the Mississippi River. Photograph by William D. Middleton.

[RIGHT] Approximately one mile west of St. Croix Tower, the bridge of the parallel Milwaukee Road main line frames a 123-car Burlington Route freight train on May 18, 1959. Just beyond the train is the Mississippi River, which the Burlington followed from Hastings to St. Paul Park. The jointly operated track between St. Paul and Hastings is still a busy line for BNSF Railway and Canadian Pacific. Photograph by William D. Middleton.

[LEFT] On August 23, 1956, the Milwaukee Road opened a new hump yard in St. Paul. At a hump yard there is a lead track on a hill (hump) over which cars are pushed. Single cars, or cars coupled in a block, are uncoupled just before or at the crest of the hump and roll by gravity into their designated tracks in an area called the classification bowl (St. Paul had thirty-five classification tracks). Mechanized pneumatic brakes called retarders controlled the speed of the cars. In this photograph the hump tower operator is lining up tracks for cars coming over the hump. The facility was still in use by Canadian Pacific in 2012. Photograph by Emil Skok; collection of John C. Luecke.

[ABOVE] This aerial view shows the yard and hump facilities on March 4, 1959. Highway 61 runs along the north side of the yard. Photograph by William D. Middleton.

[ABOVE] Willmar, ninety-one miles west of Minneapolis by rail, was a Great Northern town. As the first division point west of Minneapolis, it had a roundhouse, turntable, yard, and freight and passenger depots. It was a junction town as well, with lines radiating east to Minneapolis, west to Moorhead, southwest to Sioux City, Iowa, and northeast to St. Cloud. A set of four FT diesels, the first road diesels purchased by Great Northern in the 1940s, are passing the Willmar freight depot heading west. The lead locomotive is flying white flags, indicating it is running as an extra train, one not in the employee timetable. Action photographs of these engines in color are rare. Photograph by Perry Becker.

[RIGHT] The Minnesota Railfans Association was the most active rail enthusiast group in the state in the 1950s. On April 5, 1959, it chartered a Great Northern train from Minneapolis to Milaca for its tenth annual Diner Dinner trip. The trip brochure advised, "This will be the last opportunity to ride over the old 60-pound tracks of the Milaca Branch as the Great Northern will replace all the original rail which was laid back in 1886 with 90-pound welded rail this year and in 1960." In addition to coaches and a dining car with a menu of chicken or pike, Great Northern also provided solarium observation lounge *James J. Hill*—all for a fare of $6.75. Note the classic 1950s University of Minnesota letter sweater the passenger at the right is wearing during a photo stop a mile north of Princeton. Collection of Aaron Isaacs.

[OPPOSITE] Rolling west past the Minneapolis Cold Storage warehouse on Nicollet Island, Chicago & North Western (Omaha Road) train 63 is crossing the west channel of the Mississippi River on Great Northern track in early 1957. The train is about to pass the north side of the Great Northern Station, and in a few blocks it will swing onto the tracks of the Minneapolis & St. Louis. It will use that railroad to Merriam Junction near Shakopee, where it will finally switch onto home rails for the trip to Mankato, St. James, and Sioux City, Iowa. Rebuilt in the 1960s, this bridge is still in service and used by Northstar commuter trains as well as BNSF Railway freights. The Minneapolis Cold Storage warehouse has long since been torn down. Photograph by Charles B. McCreary.

[RIGHT] Nearing the end of a short career, Chicago & North Western's *Dakota 400* is about to cross U.S. Highway 14 at Cobden en route from Rapid City, South Dakota, to Chicago in the late 1950s. Established in 1950 between Chicago and Huron, South Dakota, and extended to Rapid City in 1955, it was the only *400* to carry sleeping cars. Service west of Mankato was discontinued in October 1960. Photograph by Perry Becker.

[ABOVE] Heading from Minneapolis to Northfield, Minneapolis, Northfield & Southern Baldwin 20 with forty-six cars rumbles past a cow pasture on September 22, 1958. The location is Savage, today a built-up suburban area of Minneapolis but in 1958 still well out in the country. Photograph by William D. Middleton.

[LEFT] The Minneapolis, Northfield & Southern made a living by moving freight around the western edge of Minneapolis to connections with the Rock Island and Milwaukee Road at Northfield and the Chicago Great Western at Randolph. Routing traffic this way allowed shippers to bypass congested yards in the Twin Cities terminal. The railroad was an early advocate of dieselization, and it purchased five heavy Baldwin Locomotive Works center cab diesels in 1948 and 1949 and another in 1953. In January 1957, center cab 24 is heading west on the Soo Line at Crystal and is about to bang over the crossing of the Great Northern line to St. Cloud. Photograph by Al Wallin; collection of John C. Luecke.

[OPPOSITE] The brakeman rides the footboard of Minneapolis, Northfield & Southern Baldwin 15 in Richfield on September 8, 1958. The brakeman's duties included ensuring that cars were coupled properly, lining switches, and signaling to the other crewmen while performing switching operations, as he is doing here. The head brakeman rode in the locomotive, and the rear brakeman rode in the caboose. Brakemen were also required to watch for signs of a hotbox, a dangerous overheating of axles that could lead to a derailment. Brakemen have largely been eliminated, although some switch jobs, where a third person is required, still use them. Photograph by William D. Middleton.

Minneapolis-based Minneapolis & St. Louis Railway's most important route was between Minneapolis and Peoria, Illinois, with other lines from Minneapolis into eastern South Dakota and various areas in north-central Iowa and south-central Minnesota. Most of its routes saw relatively light traffic. Its main business was serving as a way for shippers to bypass Chicago, routing their traffic via Peoria, where Minneapolis & St. Louis connected with several railroads and advertised itself as the "Peoria Gateway." Each evening it operated No. 20 out of Minneapolis, a priority freight train for Peoria. It is awaiting departure from the Cedar Lake Yard on October 29, 1958, with ninety-eight loads and six empties behind four diesels. Chicago & North Western purchased the 1,391-mile railroad on November 1, 1960. Photograph by William D. Middleton.

[ABOVE] In October 1958 Minneapolis & St. Louis rail diesel car 33, running as train 3 from Minneapolis to Des Moines, pauses at St. Louis Park. Minneapolis & St. Louis purchased two rail diesel cars in January 1957 named *Gopher* and *Hawkeye*. These rail diesel cars were not a success, in part because the railroad insisted on pulling cars behind them, which they were not designed to do. They also cost more to operate than older gas-electric cars. In December 1958 they were traded to the Chesapeake & Ohio Railroad for thirty-two hopper cars and were replaced with older cars until the railroad exited the passenger business in 1960. Photograph by William D. Middleton.

[RIGHT] The ancestor of today's long trains of intermodal containers were piggyback services—truck trailers being carried on railroad flatcars. A pioneer in piggyback service was Chicago Great Western, which began carrying truck trailers in 1936. In the early years of piggyback, trailers were simply driven up a ramp and onto the flatcars for loading and unloading, as demonstrated by this Minneapolis & St. Louis truck in downtown Minneapolis in October 1958. Today shipments are moved in containers and are taken on and off railroad cars using large cranes. Photograph by William D. Middleton.

The first Minnesota railroad to disappear in the 1960s was the Minneapolis & St. Louis Railway. Chicago & North Western purchased the 1,391-mile railroad on November 1, 1960. On April 24 of that year, the Minnesota Railfans Association sponsored a trip from Minneapolis to New Ulm and return. This offered passengers a chance to ride freight-only track (the portion from Winthrop to New Ulm had no passenger service). The train is swinging off the line from New Ulm onto the Minneapolis–Watertown line at Winthrop. Passenger service between Minneapolis and Watertown ended on July 20, 1960. Photograph by Perry Becker.

2
The Struggle for Survival
1960–1980

IN 1960, THE RAILROAD INDUSTRY in the United States was still healthy, but by the 1970s several roads were in bankruptcy and others were barely hanging on. One reason was the increasing losses from passenger service. To stem the tide of losses, railroads worked aggressively to discontinue passenger trains. This was aided by the Transportation Act of 1958, which gave the Interstate Commerce Commission power to authorize the discontinuance of unprofitable passenger service instead of state regulatory agencies such as the Minnesota Railroad and Warehouse Commission.[1]

In Minnesota, Minneapolis & St. Louis ended all passenger service in 1960, followed by the Chicago & North Western in 1963, Chicago Great Western in 1965, Soo Line in 1967, and Rock Island in 1969. Other railroads remained optimistic about their trains: Burlington, Great Northern, Milwaukee Road, and Northern Pacific all continued to provide excellent passenger service in the state, even as they lopped off local service on secondary routes to places such as International Falls, Duluth, and Winnipeg. After the U.S. Postal Service ended railway mail contracts in 1967, depriving passenger trains of a major source of revenue, even optimists had to face the reality that passenger trains were hemorrhaging money the railroads desperately needed.

The U.S. Congress finally addressed the "passenger train problem" in 1970. With losses mounting but with the public demanding some form of passenger train service, Congress passed the Rail Passenger Service Act of 1970, which created Amtrak, the National Railroad Passenger Corporation (NRPC). Amtrak not only saved the passenger train but also helped save the freight rail network by relieving railroads of the financial burden of running passenger trains. All eligible (noncommuter) railroads were invited to participate, and all but seven joined.

Amtrak is a public-private entity that receives taxpayer funding. It assumed operation of intercity passenger trains on May 1, 1971. Any railroad operating intercity passenger service on that date could contract with Amtrak. Participating railroads bought into Amtrak using a formula based on their recent intercity passenger train losses. The purchase price could be satisfied by either cash or rolling stock; in exchange, the railroads received common stock. Railroads that chose not to join Amtrak were required to continue operating their existing passenger service until 1975 and then had to pursue Interstate Commerce Commission approval to discontinue or alter their service.[2] Amtrak turned out to be surprisingly popular. In fiscal year 2010 the company carried 28,716,857 passengers, setting a record for the most passengers carried since it started operations.[3]

By the Amtrak takeover date of May 1, 1971, only three railroads still operated passenger trains in Minnesota: the new Burlington Northern (created by the 1970 merger of Burlington; Great Northern; Northern Pacific; and Spokane, Portland & Seattle), Canadian National, and Milwaukee Road. Canadian National operated passenger service between Winnipeg and Thunder Bay that cut through a portion of northern Minnesota near Lake of the Woods. Its single train was not worth the cost of buying into Amtrak, but Burlington Northern and Milwaukee Road joined.

Amtrak announced it would operate only one train through Minnesota, the *Empire Builder* between Chicago and Seattle. It would use the Milwaukee Road route from Chicago to St. Paul, then switch to Burlington Northern's former Great Northern line to Minneapolis, Willmar, Morris, Breckenridge, and Fargo, North Dakota. Routes that lost passenger service were St. Paul to Superior, Wisconsin; St. Paul to Fargo via St. Cloud and Detroit Lakes; St. Cloud to Fargo via Fergus Falls; Grand Forks, North Dakota, to Winnipeg via Noyes; and the former Burlington Route east of St. Paul to La Crosse and Chicago.

Amtrak chose to have only one stop in the Twin Cities and designated the Great Northern Station in Minneapolis. The Milwaukee Road Depot in Minneapolis lost its trains, as did the St. Paul Union Depot. The huge structure of the Union Depot was too costly to keep open for only a single train. It would be forty-one years before passenger trains would return.[4]

While initially Minnesota saw only one Amtrak train, that soon changed. On June 5, 1971, under pressure from Montana senator Mike Mansfield, Amtrak reinstated the *North Coast Limited* across Minnesota, North Dakota, and southern Montana. The train operated triweekly from Minneapolis to Spokane, Washington, connecting on each end with the *Empire Builder*.[5] This restored service to the communities of St. Cloud, Staples, and Detroit Lakes.

Effective with the November 14, 1971, timetable, Amtrak renamed the train *North Coast Hiawatha* and extended it east from Minneapolis to Chicago. On the days *North Coast Hiawatha* did not operate, Amtrak ran the *Hiawatha* from Minneapolis to Chicago, in effect offering twice-daily service (with the *Empire Builder*) from the Twin Cities to Chicago.[6] The *North Coast Hiawatha* was dropped in October 1979 when federal funding was withdrawn.

In 1975, a new Amtrak train came to the state, restoring service between Minneapolis and the Twin Ports, thanks to state representative Willard Munger of Duluth. By virtue of his seniority and clout with his fellow legislators, in 1973 he was able to push a bill through the Minnesota Legislature to fund a new Amtrak service between Minneapolis and Superior, Wisconsin. It took two more years for the state and Amtrak to work out all the details. The new train, dubbed the *Arrowhead* after northeastern Minnesota, left Superior in the morning, ran nonstop to Minneapolis, and returned in early evening to Superior. It connected with the *North Coast Hiawatha* in Minneapolis, offering service to and from Chicago.[7]

The *Arrowhead* entered service on April 16, 1975. On October 26, 1975, stops were added in Cambridge and Sandstone. Even with the added stops, patronage was not strong, and the legislature seemed to be cool to the train as well. Legislators seemed to buy into arguments put forth by opponents, particularly in the bus industry, that the train was being unfairly subsidized to the detriment of private competitors. In April 1976, the train was saved from extinction by a last-minute appropriation from the Legislative Advisory Commission. Over the course of the train's ten-year existence, it was in funding difficulty every year.

On February 15, 1977, two important events took place. Service directly into Duluth began when a new depot opened. More important from a ridership standpoint, the schedule was flip-flopped, with the train leaving Minneapolis in the morning and leaving Duluth in the evening. Ridership increased dramatically, particularly during the tourist season, when residents of the Twin Cities flocked to Duluth for sightseeing visits.

In its early years the *Arrowhead* connected with other Amtrak trains in Minneapolis to allow passengers to reach Chicago. In spring 1978 Amtrak combined the Duluth–Chicago and Twin Cities–Chicago trains. The new train, named the *North Star*, began service on April 30, 1978. With sleeping cars added, it traveled overnight from Chicago to St. Paul and then on the normal day schedule from St. Paul to Duluth.

Another Amtrak funding crisis occurred in 1981, and on October 26, 1981, the Chicago–Twin Cities operation and sleeper service was dropped, although the *North Star* name remained. The state of Minnesota withdrew its funding in spring 1985, and the train made its last run on Easter Sunday, April 7, 1985. Since that date Amtrak's *Empire Builder* has been the sole long-distance passenger train serving the state; Canadian National ended its service through northern Minnesota in the late 1970s.

Freight business was in decline in the 1960s and 1970s as well. As more highways were completed, the trucking industry found it easier to compete with railroads for freight traffic. While the federal government built highways and then levied fuel taxes to help pay for them, railroads continued to pay the cost of maintaining their private rights-of-way, which often included state taxes.[8]

In 1944 at the height of World War II, a record for railroad cargo carried was set at 746 billion ton-miles. In that year, 69 percent of all intercity freight ton-miles were moved by rail. From that high, railroads experienced a low point in freight traffic around 1960 when they carried less than 600 billion ton-miles of freight.[9]

Freight profits were difficult to come by, especially in the Midwest. The short distances between cities left railroads especially vulnerable to strong competition from trucks. Western railroads such as Great Northern and Northern Pacific, with their longer distances, were able to bring in more cash by moving freight farther and remained largely profitable. But by the 1960s and 1970s Midwestern railroads such as the Milwaukee Road and Rock Island were losing money. To cut costs, many railroads adopted the strategy of deferring maintenance, preserving cash by cutting back on their repair budgets. This was at best a short-term solution since eventually the trackage would have to be repaired if the company was to stay in business. Nonetheless, many railroads allowed their track structure to fall into disrepair.[10]

Another problem was that there was too much track, mostly built in the nineteenth century when the railroad industry was dominant. By the 1960s railroads in Minnesota had hundreds of miles of branch lines that generated little traffic. One railroad, the Chicago & North Western, pruned its branch line network aggressively in the 1960s and 1970s, but others, such as the Milwaukee Road, failed to do so.[11]

It was difficult to abandon a line because railroad management had to face off against the Interstate Commerce Commission, a government agency established in 1887 that tightly regulated railroads. It governed rail line abandonment cases, the termination of passenger train services, and railroad mergers. Even more significant, it had the power to determine maximum "reasonable" rail rates and required that the rates be published. As railroads lost money, the Interstate Commerce Commission was frequently an impediment to raising rates or eliminating unprofitable services.[12] Railroads sometimes had to wait years to get a ruling, the most memorable case being the pro-

posed merger of the Union Pacific with the Rock Island. In 1964, the Rock Island and Union Pacific applied to the Interstate Commerce Commission for permission to merge. That application triggered years of intra-industry fighting and bureaucratic stalling that finally ended with approval of the merger in late 1974. By that time it was too late: the Rock Island was near collapse and Union Pacific no longer wanted to merge.[13]

Despite the difficulty of getting government approval, railroads that were faced with dwindling market share and overbuilt systems sought to cut costs by merger. By merging and eliminating duplicate lines, facilities, and employees, railroads hoped they could return to profitability.[14]

In Minnesota several railroads disappeared and new ones were created. In 1960, the Chicago & North Western purchased the Minneapolis & St. Louis. Its Minneapolis headquarters was closed, but Chicago & North Western kept the Minneapolis & St. Louis Cedar Lake Shops in Minneapolis's Kenwood neighborhood. In 1961, Minneapolis-based Minneapolis, St. Paul & Sault Ste. Marie (nicknamed Soo Line) merged with the Wisconsin Central and Duluth, South Shore & Atlantic to form a new Soo Line, which adopted the nickname as its formal title. Its headquarters remained in Minneapolis. In 1968, the Chicago & North Western merged the Chicago Great Western into its system. It abandoned most of Chicago Great Western's Minnesota branch lines but operated the former Chicago Great Western main line from St. Paul to Oelwein, Iowa, and Kansas City until it acquired the parallel Rock Island route in the 1980s.[15]

By far the biggest railroad merger came in March 1970 and had a direct impact on Minnesota. James J.

Hill, the founder of the Great Northern, had long hoped to integrate the Great Northern, Northern Pacific, and the Burlington Route (owned by the two larger roads) into one large system. The government rebuffed Hill in 1904, forcing him to break up the Northern Securities Co., which controlled the three railroads. The so-called Hill Lines tried again in the 1930s with the same result.

Beginning in the late 1950s the railroads tried once more to put together a merger. Hearings were held, contracts with labor unions were negotiated, and court cases were tried. It took until 1967 for the Interstate Commerce Commission to approve the merger, which was set for May 10, 1968. Still, opposition remained, so the commission delayed implementation of the merger to allow appeals. The U.S. Department of Justice made a last-minute appeal to the Supreme Court, which finally approved the merger in early 1970. On March 2, 1970, Burlington Northern was born. The largest railroad in the United States at over twenty-three thousand miles (not including two subsidiaries), the new railroad combined the Burlington, Great Northern, Northern Pacific, and Spokane, Portland & Seattle railways and was based in St. Paul.[16]

Burlington Northern was one of only a few railroad success stories in the 1970s. The same year Burlington Northern was formed, another railroad, Penn Central, went bankrupt. At the time it was the largest corporate bankruptcy ever in the United States. It had been created on February 1, 1968, by the merger of the New York Central and Pennsylvania railroads, with the New Haven added by government order on December 31, 1968.

Unlike Burlington Northern, whose managers came from similar corporate cultures and had long planned the integration of their systems, the Penn Central merger was a disaster from the start. The railroads were historic rivals with parallel systems, heavy passenger and commuter train traffic, incompatible computer systems, expensive union contracts, and vastly different operating practices. It declared bankruptcy on June 21, 1970.[17] Several other eastern railroads fell to bankruptcy as well. In 1976, the Penn Central and several other Eastern railroads were effectively nationalized with the creation of Conrail, which eventually became profitable, was privatized, and sold and split up between CSX Transportation and Norfolk Southern in 1999.[18]

While Conrail brought a solution to the rail problem in the Northeast, in the mid-1970s two railroads that served Minnesota went bankrupt. The seven-thousand-mile Chicago, Rock Island & Pacific (Rock Island Lines) declared bankruptcy on March 17, 1975, with the Milwaukee Road following on December 19, 1977.[19]

The Rock Island attempted to reorganize on its own, but on August 28, 1979, its clerks went on strike in a dispute over wages, followed by the members of the United Transportation Union. President Jimmy Carter appointed an emergency board to settle the dispute. United Transportation Union members came back to work, but the Brotherhood of Railway and Airline Clerks stayed off the job. By order of the Interstate Commerce Commission, the Kansas City Terminal Railway took over Rock Island operations on September 26, 1979. In early 1980, the bankruptcy court determined that the Rock Island could not be reorganized and ordered the liquidation of the railroad, the largest such liquidation in U.S. history.[20] On March 31, 1980, the Rock Island operated its last trains. However, nearly all of Rock Island's major routes were sold to other railroads, including the main line from St. Paul to Albert Lea and Des Moines, purchased by the Chicago & North Western in 1983. The North Western had leased the line from the Rock's trustee beginning on April 1, 1980.[21]

The trustee of the Milwaukee Road put forth a reorganization plan in 1979 that called for the abandonment of the lines between Montana and the Pacific Coast and branch lines in the West and Midwest. By cutting off these lines management could concentrate on the remaining core railroad in the Midwest. Congress passed the Milwaukee Road Restructuring Act on November 2, 1979, which gave the bankruptcy court the power to decide which Milwaukee Road lines could be abandoned instead of the Interstate Commerce Commission. It also provided as much as $75 million in funds for employee protection.

The Milwaukee Road embargo went into effect on February 29, 1980. In Minnesota the embargoed lines were between La Crescent and Austin; Austin to Mason City, Iowa; Farmington to Mankato; Jackson to Madison, South Dakota; and from La Crescent to Marquette, Iowa. The Marquette and Mason City lines later reopened. In March 1982 the railroad cut back farther from Miles City, Montana, to Ortonville, with the line sold to the State of South Dakota. The strategy of cutting down to a core railroad worked: in March 1982 the slimmed-down three-thousand-mile system earned its first profit, a net income of $4.2 million. The Soo Line purchased the Milwaukee Road in 1985.[22]

If there was one bright spot in the railroad picture over the twenty-year period between 1960 and 1980, it was the dramatic increase in coal traffic. The main beneficiary was Burlington Northern, which happened to have lines that sat along huge seams of coal in Montana and Wyoming. Demand for coal was driven up by the passage of the Clean Air Act of 1970, which required coal-burning power plants to reduce sulphur emissions. The subbituminous coal along Burlington Northern's lines in Montana and Wyoming has a sulphur content that's nearly four-fifths less than coal mined in the eastern United States.[23]

To move coal, Burlington Northern and other railroads had to rebuild their track infrastructure. Coal is a heavy commodity that can easily damage track if it is not properly maintained. Burlington Northern, led by Louis W. Menk and Robert W. Downing, was able to persuade its board of directors to move ahead with track overhauls, add new tracks, and spend $113 million to build a new coal line in Wyoming that opened in 1979.[24] Just how big was this coal boom? In 1970, the new Burlington Northern carried just 3 million tons of coal; in 1981, the railroad moved 112.1 million tons.[25]

Two Minnesota companies were early users of low-sulphur coal shipped by rail. On May 1, 1969, Minnesota Power & Light began receiving shipments of Montana coal at its Clay Boswell Plant at Cohasset. Trains moved over the Northern Pacific 580 miles from Montana's Big Sky Mine to Moorhead, where they were handed off to Great Northern for delivery to Cohasset. These trains marked the beginning of Burlington Northern as a major coal hauler even before the merger had taken place and were the forerunners of thousands of unit coal trains to follow.[26]

Northern States Power began receiving coal in the 1970s at its High Bridge Plant in St. Paul, Riverside Plant in Minneapolis, and later at plants in Burnsville and Bayport served by Chicago & North Western.

In 1984, with the aid of Union Pacific, the Chicago & North Western entered the Wyoming coalfields to compete with Burlington Northern directly. By Interstate Commerce Commission order, it paid Burlington Northern for half the cost of the new Wyoming coal line.[27] It's safe to say that without coal trains, the 1960s and 1970s would have been even bleaker for railroads.

Railroads hold a unique place in the American psyche. They helped build the nation in the nineteenth century and then served as the primary mode of transportation in the first half of the twentieth century. The large steam locomotives that once powered the trains and the sleek passenger trains that once moved millions are pleasant memories for thousands of Americans. Some of them became lifelong railroad fans and moved beyond mere memories to take an active role in the preservation of railroad history. Preservation-minded individuals in Duluth and the Twin Cities were responsible for preserving equipment and establishing railroad museums, even as many railroads were struggling for survival.

In the Twin Cities, the Minnesota Transportation Museum was an outgrowth of the Minnesota Railfans Association, which organized dozens of excursion trips in the 1950s and 1960s. The association played a key role in preserving Northern Pacific 4-6-0 No. 328 in 1950. It once worked on Northern Pacific's Wyoming to Taylors Falls branch. No. 368 was placed in a Stillwater Park in 1954.

The Minnesota Railfans Association also sponsored several trips over the Twin City Rapid Transit Company's streetcar lines until the last of the system was abandoned in 1954. The organization was able to save streetcar 1300, built in 1908, and stored it until 1962, when title was passed to the newly established Minnesota Transportation Museum. The new museum also acquired Soo Line 0-6-0 No. 353 from Koppers Coke (which it sold in 1972), a Northern Pacific coach, and Dan Patch Lines 100, the first successful internal combustion locomotive, built in 1913.

In 1971 the museum restored a portion of Twin City Rapid Transit Company right-of-way along Lake Harriet in Minneapolis and began operating car 1300. Several other cars were restored over the years (the streetcars are now part of the Minnesota Streetcar Museum, created in December 2004 as part of a restructuring of the Minnesota Transportation Museum, which spun off its streetcar operations). Northern Pacific 328 came to the museum in 1976, when it leased the engine from the City of Stillwater. Restoration work began at a building at Burlington Northern's Como Shops in St. Paul, which the museum leased beginning in 1973. No. 328 began excursion operations in 1981. The museum also acquired another Northern Pacific steam locomotive, 4-6-2 No. 2156, which was donated to the City of St. Paul in 1954 and displayed at Como Park, although it has not yet been restored.

While the Minnesota Transportation Museum engaged in restoration and operations at several sites in the Twin Cities, in Duluth efforts were underway to preserve the Union Depot, a Duluth landmark, and install a railroad museum at track level. The Boston firm of Peabody & Stearns designed the Union Depot with large twin turrets in French Norman style. Opened in 1892, the building once served trains of the Duluth, Missabe & Iron Range and its predecessors Duluth & Iron Range and Duluth, Missabe & Northern; Duluth, Superior & Western (later Great Northern); Great Northern; Northern Pacific; St. Paul & Duluth; and Duluth, South Shore & Atlantic. In its heyday between 1910 and 1920, fifty trains served the depot daily. A Northern Pacific rail diesel car to Staples, which departed on May 24, 1969, was the last passenger train to use the building.

As the depot was losing its trains, a Cultural Center Committee was set up to investigate ways to establish a museum and cultural center in the city. The committee looked at the Union and Soo Line depots and settled on the Union Depot as its preferred site. The Area Cultural Committee purchased the depot and surrounding trackage from Burlington Northern in 1971, the same year it was designated a National Historic Site. It is now the property of St. Louis County.

In 1973 the Lake Superior Museum of Transportation & Industry was incorporated (the name was changed to Lake Superior Railroad Museum on December 1, 1997). Funding for the initial construction of the museum came from a federal grant of $352,000 and $88,000 in private donations—the original cost of building the depot, from 1890 to 1892, was $615,027.

One of the main backers of the railroad museum was Donald B. Shank, vice president and general manager of the Duluth, Missabe & Iron Range Railway. Shank prevailed on his colleagues from the railroads that came into the Twin Ports to serve on the board of directors. Board members in turn went to their railroads to obtain equipment for the museum, run fund-raising excursions, and move equipment to the museum free of charge. Often railroads would overhaul a piece before it was donated so the museum would not have the labor and expense of restoring equipment.

Shank was the man in charge of bringing the largest artifact to the museum: Duluth, Missabe & Iron Range 2-8-8-4 Yellowstone steam locomotive 227, built in 1941. It is 128 feet long and weighs 566 tons in working condition. Restored by the Duluth, Missabe & Iron Range, the locomotive was placed in the museum in 1974. The wheels on the 227 are powered by electric motors that allow the engine to "run" every half hour. An audio system features recorded sounds of the engine in operation in the late 1950s.

Another notable in the collection is Minnesota's first locomotive, St. Paul & Pacific 1, the *William Crooks,* built in 1861. It made the first run of a Minnesota railroad between St. Paul and St. Anthony (which later became part of Minneapolis) on June 28, 1862. Also displayed is Northern Pacific's first locomotive, the *Minnetonka,* built in 1870. It was used in the building of the Northern Pacific, which began construction of its transcontinental line twenty-five miles from Duluth at Thompson Junction (now Carlton) on February 15, 1870.

Even as efforts were underway to preserve Minnesota's railroad heritage in the 1970s, the future of Minnesota railroading was still in doubt as several railroads struggled. No one could predict it, but the railroads of Minnesota, and the railroad industry in the United States, were on the verge of a remarkable renaissance.

Steam was on its way out on the Duluth, Missabe & Iron Range in 1960, but railroad fans made sure the end didn't go unnoticed. On July 3, 1960, the Illini Railroad Club and Minnesota Railfans Association sponsored a trip over the Duluth, Missabe & Iron Range from Duluth to Ely/Winton using Yellowstone steam locomotive 222. The train is departing Duluth Union Depot, passing a string of wooden Northern Pacific refrigerator cars. The Hotel Spalding looms over the scene. Over the next decade the face of downtown Duluth would change radically with old buildings demolished and new ones rising in their place. Photograph by Perry Becker; courtesy of the Missabe Road Historical Society.

It's almost 4:00 p.m. at the Soo Line dispatcher's office in the depot at Thief River Falls on May 8, 1961. Dispatcher Bill Walters is smiling, but when the clock strikes four, the office will close and the dispatcher's duties will be transferred to offices in Enderlin, North Dakota, and at Shoreham Yard in Minneapolis. Train dispatchers like Walters are responsible for coordinating the use of tracks within the area they supervise. They are responsible for deciding when trains get to use which tracks and for allocating tracks so they are used as efficiently as possible. Today dispatchers use computerized systems to monitor and control trains and to communicate directly with train crews. The desk in this photograph was scratch-built by Shoreham Shop forces and was later purchased by photographer Stuart Nelson as a memento of his years dispatching for Soo and successor Canadian Pacific. Photograph by Stuart J. Nelson.

The railroad depot was once the center of activity in cities and towns across Minnesota. Residents traveled on passenger trains, sent telegrams via Western Union, and received packages from Railway Express at the depot. By the 1960s, the importance of the depot had declined as residents switched to private automobiles, passenger service ended, and truckers captured less-than-carload freight business. Looking worn by decades of use, the depot at Eyota on Chicago & North Western's Winona–Rapid City line stands along well-maintained track in June 1963. Eyota was a junction town, with branch lines north to Plainview and south to Chatfield. Photograph by Baron Behning.

Duluth, Winnipeg & Pacific rail diesel car service between Duluth and Fort Frances, Ontario, begun in 1957, was short-lived. It ceased operation on July 1, 1961, with the car moving to parent Canadian National. Train 620 from Fort Frances is arriving at the West Duluth depot in 1961. The depot was located on a large wood trestle that carried the tracks above city streets. Photograph by Wayne C. Olsen; collection of Lake Superior Railroad Museum.

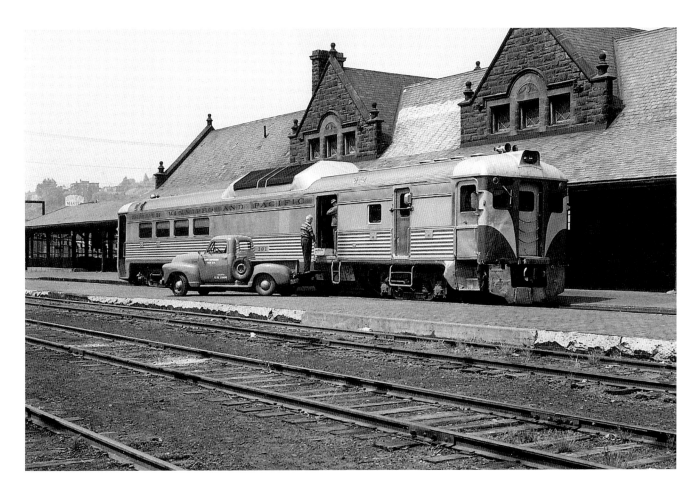

On June 26, 1961, just four days before the end of Duluth, Winnipeg & Pacific passenger service, car D-301 has arrived at the Omaha Road depot in downtown Duluth, where a Lake Superior Fish Company truck has pulled up to unload boxes of fish. After the cessation of passenger service, the Omaha Road depot was demolished, and today portions of Interstate Highway 35 cover the site. Photograph by C. F. Sager; collection of James Kreuzberger, Minnesota Streetcar Museum.

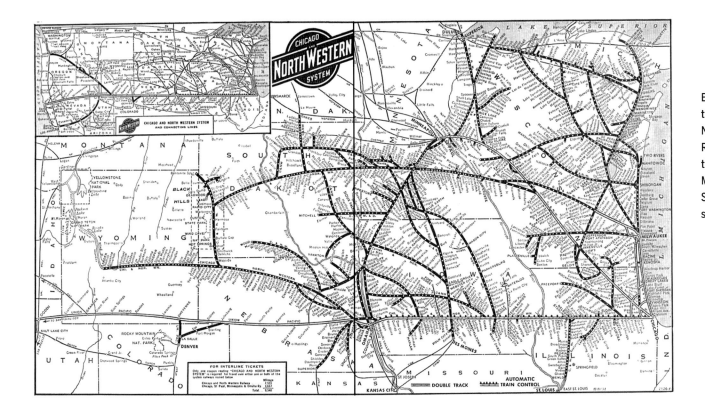

Before mergers expanded its reach in the 1950s and 1960s, the Chicago & North Western and subsidiary Omaha Road formed a Midwest railroad system that served nine states: Illinois, Iowa, Minnesota, Nebraska, North Dakota, South Dakota, Upper Michigan, Wisconsin, and Wyoming. Author's collection.

[OPPOSITE, ABOVE] Throughout the 1950s, the Chicago & North Western steadily pared down its passenger service in Minnesota. After June 1959, the only North Western train serving Minneapolis/St. Paul was the *Twin Cities 400,* which still looked prosperous as it crossed the Stone Arch Bridge in Minneapolis in June 1961. However, looks can be deceiving; in 1961 the train lost $1,187,240, or $3.59 per mile. The construction equipment gathered below the bridge is working on a new Mississippi River lock, which required the removal of two of the stone arches. A steel truss replaced them so barges could pass through. Photograph by Byron D. Olsen.

[OPPOSITE, BELOW] In March 1962, the *400* bangs over the crossing with the Milwaukee Road at Lakeland Junction and heads onto the St. Croix River swing bridge to enter Wisconsin at Hudson. Photograph by Bill Graham; collection of Aaron Isaacs.

[RIGHT] In October 1960, the Chicago–Rapid City, South Dakota, *Dakota 400* was dropped west of Mankato, and the remaining service was renamed the *Rochester 400*. On July 23, 1963, both the *Rochester 400* and the *Twin Cities 400* were discontinued, ending Chicago & North Western passenger service in the state. A little over a month before the end, the *Rochester 400* slows for the stop at the brick depot in St. Charles on June 9, 1963. Photograph by Baron Behning.

[ABOVE] The pride of the Great Northern, the *Empire Builder,* races east out of Willmar on a wintry day in the early 1960s. The orange and green streamliner is running late this day—it normally departed Willmar in the wee hours of the morning. The *Empire Builder* included shorter dome coaches and a full-length dome—the only streamliner to carry both dome types. Great Northern president John Budd believed that as long as his railroad ran passenger trains, it should run them properly. Photograph by Perry Becker.

[OPPOSITE] In 1966, Great Northern's *Winnipeg Limited* glides downgrade at Westminster Tower in St. Paul. The *Limited* provided overnight service between the Twin Cities and the Manitoba capital carrying a sleeper and a buffet-lounge car. It also carried mail and, on this day, a flatcar with two truckloads of freight, referred to as piggyback trailers. Photograph by Byron D. Olsen.

On board the *Empire Builder,* passengers could make reservations for different dinner seating times and would receive this card as confirmation. Author's collection.

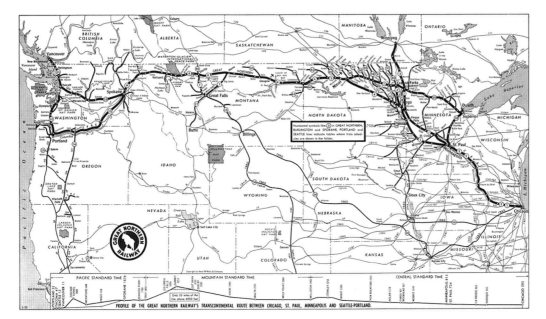

Based in St. Paul, the legendary Great Northern Railway was the work of "Empire Builder" James J. Hill, who extended the railroad's reach from the Midwest to Puget Sound and into Canada. In 1931 the railroad opened a new line to Northern California in conjunction with Western Pacific. Author's collection.

[OPPOSITE] Despite the loss of passengers in the 1960s, Great Northern remained stubbornly optimistic. It continued to advertise its trains, ran specials for groups, kept service levels high, and purchased newer secondhand equipment to replace older cars. Great Northern provided twice-daily service between the Twin Cities and the Twin Ports with its *Badger* and *Gopher* passenger trains, named for the state animals of Wisconsin and Minnesota. On July 23, 1963 (the same day Chicago & North Western's *Twin Cities 400* made its last run), the southbound *Gopher* is passing the depot at Brook Park, approximately halfway between Duluth and St. Paul. Photograph by Baron Behning.

[ABOVE] It's a busy July morning in 1964 as an ore boat approaches the Duluth, Missabe & Iron Range's Duluth Docks, where at least three other boats are already tied up. In the foreground is Great Northern's *Badger* from the Twin Cities crossing the drawbridge over St. Louis Bay. The *Gopher* and *Badger,* by then down to one round-trip daily, made their last runs in 1971. The drawbridge was locked open for the last time at noon on June 1, 1984. Photograph by William D. Middleton.

[OPPOSITE] Great Northern brought a new look to railroading in 1967 with the introduction of Big Sky Blue colors that replaced the orange and green scheme introduced in the early 1940s. To show off the new image, Great Northern assembled a train of 114 new jumbo grain hoppers and dispatched it west from Minneapolis. Led by two 3,600-horsepower SD45s and a single SDP45, the train is rolling through Dead Man's Curve two miles west of Delano on August 2, 1967. The curve got its nickname after a head-on collision between a westbound snowplow extra and an eastbound passenger train in the 1920s. Photograph by Great Northern Railway; courtesy of the Minnesota Historical Society.

[ABOVE] While many mourned the loss of the traditional orange paint scheme, Great Northern's new colors really stood out among the greenery of the railroad's service area. Three Big Sky Blue F7 diesels, and another in orange, bring a loaded ore train east at the Minnesota–Wisconsin state line near Wrenshall on September 11, 1971. This is a Burlington Northern train, but the diesels have yet to be repainted in Burlington Northern's Cascade Green colors. Collection of Mark R. Lynn.

Great Northern founder James J. Hill believed in making constant improvement to his properties. His successors continued that tradition, rebuilding and improving track and structures and buying new equipment. As the diesels that had replaced steam aged, a second generation of power emerged. As a railroad that took its public image seriously, Great Northern made sure to show off its new locomotives. In June 1969 it hosted an equipment display at the Minnesota State Fairgrounds in St. Paul. No. 2539, a General Electric 3,300 horsepower U33C, is open for inspection on the track across Como Avenue from the main gate of the Fairgrounds. Photograph by Byron D. Olsen.

MOBILE HOME...

GREAT NORTHERN'S EMPIRE BUILDER—your mobile home —gets you where you're going—carefree, relaxed—and you live a little along the way.

Plenty of room to move around. Roomy Day-Nite coaches with stretch-out seats and Great Dome "penthouse" seats topside, or a choice of cozy sleeping accommodations. The Ranch Lounge for meals and beverages. Picture-window views of the Rockies in Glacier National Park.

The Empire Builder dining car—crisp linen, attractive china, glistening silver and glassware, and delicious food prepared to your order. The Empire Builder two-level, full-length dome-lounge car is great for sociability, refreshments and views.

Every day each way between Chicago and Seattle-Portland via Spokane. Westbound, leaves St. Paul at 8:35 P.M., leaves Minneapolis at 9:05 P.M.

GREAT NORTHERN

[ABOVE, LEFT] Long after most railroads had thrown in the towel on passenger service, Great Northern still marketed its *Empire Builder* passenger train. This ad ran in Twin Cities newspapers in the late 1960s, touting the *Empire Builder* as a traveler's "mobile home." The full-length dome and passenger cars are wearing Great Northern's new Big Sky Blue colors adopted in 1967. Author's collection.

[ABOVE, RIGHT] Here's the view an engineer had bringing a Milwaukee Road passenger train into the St. Paul Union Depot from the east in the early 1960s. The train had to negotiate the depot's maze of tracks into the platforms, where it stopped before heading to the Milwaukee Road Depot in Minneapolis. Chicago Great Western, Milwaukee Road, Rock Island, and some Omaha Road and Soo Line trains had it easy—they just ran through the depot. The trains of other lines had to back in or out, or they originated or terminated at the depot. Photograph by Emil Skok; collection of John C. Luecke.

[RIGHT] In the passenger train era, railroads seldom missed a chance to get their name in front of the public. The Soo Line handed out these eyeglass tissues on their passenger trains, telling passengers to "ship and travel Soo." Author's collection.

SOO LINE RAILROAD

$OO $INE

Clean your glasses
Shine 'em too,
You will have a smile
If you ship and travel Soo

Soo Line was never a major passenger carrier, but the few trains it did run were known for quality service. One such train was the overnight *Winnipeger* between the Twin Cities and Winnipeg, a direct competitor of Great Northern's *Winnipeg Limited*. Great Northern had a more direct route and streamlined cars while Soo stuck with older sleepers and coaches. The train was a big mail and express carrier, as can be seen at Hamel on June 23, 1963, as the eastbound train blasts through town. The mail contract was terminated in June 1965, and the *Winnipeger* made its last run on March 24, 1967. Photograph by Baron Behning.

How the New Soo works for you

When the Minneapolis, St. Paul & Sault Ste. Marie, the Duluth, South Shore & Atlantic, and the Wisconsin Central merged in 1961, the new company dubbed itself the "New Soo." It issued this brochure, featuring a photograph of a train crossing the St. Croix River High Bridge from Wisconsin into Minnesota. Author's collection.

In the 1950s and 1960s the Soo Line provided passenger service between the Twin Cities and Chicago via a train that connected with the Duluth–Chicago *Laker* at Owen, Wisconsin. On a July 1964 evening it is departing St. Paul on the Northern Pacific, leaving the tunnel under the Chicago & North Western and passing Northern Pacific's Mississippi Street locomotive shop. In about a mile it will swing onto home rails at Soo Line Junction. Color photographs of this train with red and white (actually light gray) diesels are rare, since Soo did not adopt these colors until 1962 and the train was discontinued in 1965. Photograph by Byron D. Olsen.

Action at the Milwaukee Road Depot in Minneapolis finds Soo Line's *Winnipeger* preparing to leave the depot on the last lap of its 464-mile run from Winnipeg to St. Paul in 1962. Behind the locomotive is a baggage car from parent Canadian Pacific. The Canadian carrier owned 56 percent of the common stock of the Soo Line, although it allowed the Soo to operate independently until it purchased all remaining stock in 1990. Photograph by Byron D. Olsen.

The *Afternoon Hiawatha* awaits its departure from Minneapolis for Chicago in 1965 as a Rock Island train arrives at the Milwaukee Road Depot. The *Afternoon Hiawatha* never suffered downgrading, as did many other passenger trains in the 1960s. It remained a class operation carrying a diner, Super Dome, and distinctive Skytop-parlor observation car until its last run on January 23, 1970. It was the last passenger train serving the state to carry an observation car. Photograph by Byron D. Olsen.

[ABOVE] Inside the Minneapolis Milwaukee Road Depot in August 1968, the sad state of railroad passenger service is evident: only two people are at the ticket counter, and a single individual waits for a train. Photograph by David Meppen; collection of John C. Luecke.

[OPPOSITE] Engineer Al Bloom and fireman Bill Hellenberg engage in the time-honored tradition of comparing their watches prior to taking the *Afternoon Hiawatha* out of the Milwaukee Road Depot. It was always important that crew members kept the same time throughout a passenger run. Before a trip and when reporting to duty on a given day, all operating crew members (conductor, engineer, trainmen, fireman) set their watches to a standard clock maintained to accurate standard time by the railroad at the office where employees signed in each day. Customarily, the conductor and engineer compared watches just before departure. Photograph by Emil Skok; collection of John C. Luecke.

[ABOVE] Flying high above downtown Minneapolis on March 7, 1968, photographer Robert McCoy captured this bird's-eye view of the Minneapolis Milwaukee Road Depot and surrounding area. McCoy was contracted by the Milwaukee Road to take aerial photographs of the system. The *Afternoon Hiawatha* is in the station, waiting for a 12:15 p.m. departure. The Great Northern Station is visible in the far upper left along the Mississippi River, and the west end of Great Northern's Stone Arch Bridge can be seen at the upper right. The area was a maze of railroad tracks in 1968, but none remain today. Photograph by Robert McCoy; collection of Nathan Molldrem.

[OPPOSITE] McCoy's airplane is south of downtown Minneapolis, looking down at Hiawatha Avenue (*center*). Just east of Hiawatha is the sprawling facilities of Minneapolis-Moline, manufacturers of farm equipment such as the Minnie-Mo tractor. The company was an important Milwaukee Road shipper; the railroad brought in supplies for manufacturing and moved out finished equipment. The plant closed in 1972. To the north is the Milwaukee Road's South Minneapolis Yard; only a circle of concrete remains where a huge roundhouse once stood. Except for tracks south of Lake Street, nothing remains of the railroad in this area today, although the Hiawatha Light Rail Line crosses above Lake Street and parallels Hiawatha Avenue. Photograph by Robert McCoy; collection of Nathan Molldrem.

Another large Milwaukee Road shipper was the Ford Plant in St. Paul's Highland Park neighborhood. The complex opened in 1924, complete with a dam on the Mississippi River to generate hydroelectric power for the facility. The Milwaukee Road constructed a spur track off its Short Line just west of downtown to service the plant. Looking west at the complex on March 7, 1968, the large yard is visible, with a diesel switch engine just east of the Cleveland Avenue overpass. The Ford Parkway Bridge is at upper right, and Lock and Dam No. 1 is just to the south. Across the river is Minnehaha Park. The Ford Plant closed in December 2011. Photograph by Robert McCoy; collection of Nathan Molldrem.

Sacks of mail wait to be loaded as Northern Pacific train 2, the *Main-streeter,* slides into the depot at Manitoba Junction east of Hawley on July 17, 1963. Passengers could connect here with a rail diesel car to Winnipeg. The *Mainstreeter,* a play on Northern Pacific's slogan "Main Street of the Northwest," was established in 1952 when Northern Pacific's flag-ship *North Coast Limited* was given a faster schedule. The *Mainstreeter* took over local stops skipped by the faster train and also handled mail and express. After the mail contract was lost in the late 1960s, Northern Pacific tried to get rid of the train, but it hung on until the advent of Amtrak in 1971. Photograph by Baron Behning.

Winnipeg-bound rail diesel car 124 is loading passengers and mail at Hawley in July 1966. The car began its run in Fargo, heading east on the Northern Pacific main line to Manitoba Junction before turning north for Canada. Car B-32 was originally built for the Western Pacific Railroad and was sold to Northern Pacific in 1962. Northern Pacific passenger service to Winnipeg ended on May 24, 1969. Collection of Aaron Isaacs.

[LEFT] Railroads employed thousands of workers for tasks ranging from rebuilding locomotives and building bridges to more mundane jobs such as washing equipment. Back in the days when railroads took pride in their appearance, a Northern Pacific employee scrubs down a rail diesel car at Staples. Today most railroads wash their locomotives only when they come into a shop for maintenance, mainly because of environmental rules that prohibit the use of the chemicals that are needed to clean the grimy equipment. Northern Pacific offered twice-daily rail diesel car service between Duluth and Staples, where the cars connected with the *North Coast Limited* and *Mainstreeter*. One of these cars was the last passenger train out of the Duluth Union Depot in May 1969. Photograph by William D. Middleton.

[BELOW] The Northern Pacific billed itself as the "Main Street of the Northwest" because its main route extended from the Twin Cities and Twin Ports to Seattle and Portland. Author's collection.

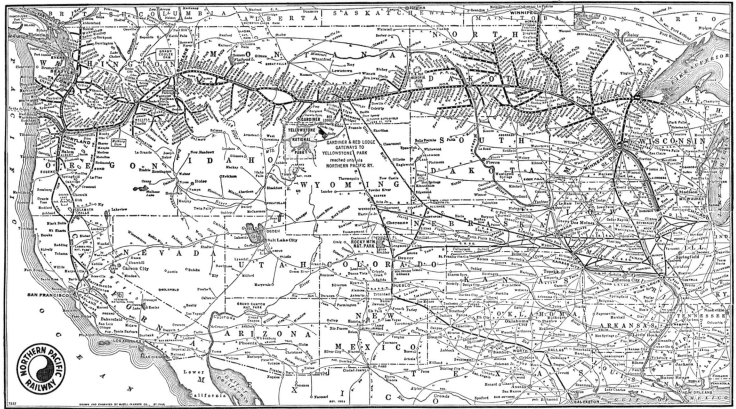

NORTHERN PACIFIC RAILWAY --------------------- *Main Street of the Northwest*

Not only did passenger equipment need a good scrubbing, but freight cars did as well. Depending on the type of shipment, a dirty car could contaminate the contents, spoiling the cargo and costing the railroad money. A good example is rolled finished paper produced by paper mills. A dirty boxcar can ruin the paper, so companies will reject cars if they aren't clean. This crew of Great Northern workers is cleaning boxcars at the company's shop at Waite Park near St. Cloud. Photograph for Great Northern by Hedrich-Blessing Studio, Minnesota Historical Society Collection.

The transition from steam to diesel was complete by the 1960s, but there were still a few isolated steam operations. One was in the Midway area of St. Paul, where in the early 1960s the Koppers Coke Company employed two secondhand Soo Line 0-6-0s in switching service. The contrast couldn't be greater as three new Chicago & North Western GP30s pass Koppers Coke 0-6-0 No. 353. The steam locomotive was built in 1920 for the Soo Line and is switching the yard just west of the Koppers plant in St. Paul. No. 353 still runs in 2012, pulling trains filled with visitors on a circle of track around the grounds of the Western Minnesota Steam Threshers Reunion at Rollag each Labor Day weekend. Photograph by Perry Becker.

In the early 1960s Minnesota fans of big steam locomotives relied on the occasional visits of Burlington 4-8-4 No. 5632 to satisfy their craving for steam. The locomotive was used in excursion service though 1964 and was scheduled for a major rebuild in 1965. A change in Burlington management put an end to the steam program, and in 1967 No. 5632 was sold. In a tragedy for the rail preservation community, the locomotive was scrapped in 1976 in a dispute over storage payments. In the heyday of Burlington's steam program, No. 5632 speeds past Milwaukee Road's Pig's Eye Yard in St. Paul in a blur of steam and steel. Photograph by Perry Becker.

CHICAGO GREAT WESTERN RAILWAY

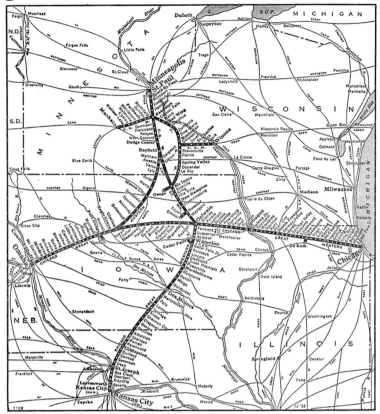

[LEFT] The Chicago Great Western advertised itself as the "Corn Belt Route" serving Iowa, Illinois, Minnesota, Missouri, and Nebraska. In the years following its 1968 merger with Chicago & North Western, nearly all of its main lines were abandoned. Author's collection.

[BELOW] When the Chicago Great Western made the move to diesels, it turned to Electro-Motive's F models. The railroad was known for assembling tremendously long trains pulled by strings of these streamlined diesels, sometimes assembling up to eight or more on a single train. On May 14, 1966, at least five Fs are passing the depot at Kenyon. Chicago Great Western merged with Chicago & North Western on July 1, 1968, but the practice of coupling long strings of these locomotives together continued until 1976, when most of the Fs were stricken from the Chicago & North Western motive power roster. Photograph by William Cordes, Minnesota Streetcar Museum Collection.

Chicago Great Western 52 drags a local freight west out of Cannon Falls on the line between Red Wing and Randolph in early 1964. Progressive Rail now operates this line. The Mill Towns Trail is being constructed near the Progressive Rail right-of-way between Cannon Falls and Northfield. The Chicago Great Western main line was constructed later than many Minnesota railroads and built its reputation as a bridge line carrying freight handed off from other lines. From the Twin Cities its main line headed south to Oelwein, Iowa, where lines fanned out to Chicago, Des Moines, and Kansas City. Chicago Great Western merged into Chicago & North Western on July 1, 1968. Photograph by Oscar Palrud; collection of Aaron Isaacs.

Eight years after the Chicago Great Western merged into the Chicago & North Western, it appears that nothing has changed. No. 52 still wears its red Chicago Great Western colors crossing the Cannon River with an eastbound local at Cannon Falls on January 9, 1976. The bridge was removed in 1995. Photograph by Steve Glischinski.

[OPPOSITE, ABOVE] By 1969 the Chicago & North Western and Soo Line had dropped all passenger service in Minnesota, and on July 25, the Rock Island joined them. The final run of the *Plainsman* is arriving in St. Paul from Minneapolis. After the northbound *Plainsman* arrives that evening, the Rock Island would run only freight in the Gopher State. The diesels were recently purchased from Union Pacific and still wear Union Pacific's yellow colors. Photograph by Byron D. Olsen.

[OPPOSITE, BELOW] The Chicago, Rock Island & Pacific (Rock Island) was famed in song as a "mighty fine line" but was on a long decline in the 1960s. It earned its last profit in 1965, pursued a merger with Union Pacific that dragged on for ten years but was never consummated, and cut expenditures on maintenance and passenger service. Its last Minnesota passenger train was the daytime Minneapolis–Kansas City *Plainsman*, created in October 1966 when the Minneapolis–Fort Worth *Twin Star Rocket* was eliminated south of Kansas City. *The Plainsman* seems to be doing good business as the fireman waves to passengers as it pulls into Albert Lea from Kansas City. Photograph by David Meppen; collection of John C. Luecke.

[ABOVE] The engineer's-eye view available from a dome car is aptly demonstrated in this photograph from August 1969. We're on board Burlington's *Morning Zephyr* departing St. Paul Union Depot for Minneapolis. Photographer Tom Carlson has grabbed a seat in the first row of the Zephyr's dome car, known as the "railfan's seat" for its unobstructed forward view. As the streamliner curves out of the depot and under Kellogg Boulevard, it meets Northern Pacific train 2, the *Mainstreeter* from Seattle and Portland, dropping down Westminster Hill into the depot. Photograph by Tom Carlson.

[BELOW] By the late 1960s, only the Burlington Route, Great Northern, and Northern Pacific still served the Minneapolis Great Northern Station. Tickets were issued at the station with the logos of the three railroads. Author's collection.

Short lines are an important part of Minnesota railroading. One of the most famous was the Duluth & Northeastern. Based in Cloquet, it served the paper mill of its owner, Potlatch Corporation, and was once a logging railroad that stretched nearly to the Canadian border. The logging track was abandoned in 1941, but Duluth & Northeastern retained a fourteen-mile segment from Cloquet to Saginaw to connect with the Duluth, Missabe & Iron Range. It was one of the last railroads to operate steam locomotives, keeping some in service until 1964. Its shops were a throwback to the era when steam ruled the rails. Duluth & Northeastern 16 is parked at the Cloquet shops on October 7, 1961. Photograph by Richard Thompson.

Duluth & Northeastern 16 blasts smoke skyward as it challenges Saginaw Hill south of its namesake city on June 2, 1962. The hill ran for approximately two miles, beginning west of the Highway 33 crossing and continuing into Saginaw. To make sure the train would not stall, a brakeman would sometimes ride the front of the locomotive and unload on the run to align the Saginaw Yard switch so the train would not have to stop. Engine 16 was built new for Duluth & Northeastern in 1913 and is on display at Fauley Park in Cloquet, not far from the tracks it once operated over. Photograph by Richard Thompson.

[ABOVE] As the railroad integrated its properties, predecessor diesels mixed it up on Burlington Northern trains. At Milaca in July 1971, locomotives that once served the Great Northern and Northern Pacific are bringing the St. Cloud–Brook Park turn by the depot. This line was abandoned in 1983. Photograph by Tom Carlson.

[OPPOSITE] In a scene as old as railroading, Duluth & Northeastern 2-8-0 No. 14 takes on water from the frozen tank at Cloquet. Water tanks were located in terminals and spaced at points along the railroad at the approximate distance a steam locomotive could travel before the tender would run out of of water. No. 14, built for Duluth & Northeastern by Baldwin in 1913, was preserved. After several ownership changes, it was purchased by Southern California's Fillmore & Western Railway and restored to operation in 2010. Photograph by William D. Middleton.

[ABOVE, RIGHT] The new Burlington Northern was a consolidation of three railroads that served Minnesota: the Burlington Route, Great Northern, and Northern Pacific. The railroad also included the Pacific Northwest's Spokane, Portland & Seattle. The railroad had a large yard facility in Dilworth, whose residents recognized the railroad with this sign that greeted motorists on Highway 10 in the 1970s. Photograph by Steve Glischinski.

[OPPOSITE, ABOVE] Burlington Northern adopted Cascade Green as its color of choice for the merged railroads, since it represented the forest country of the Pacific Northwest as well as the timber industry, one of the railroad's major customers. Burlington Northern repainted its entire fleet of nearly two thousand engines in only seven years; the last engine rolled out of the paint shops on September 9, 1977. Four ex–Northern Pacific F9 diesels in Burlington Northern paint rumble across the Mississippi River at Brainerd on October 2, 1977. Photograph by Dan Poitras; collection of Tom Carlson.

[OPPOSITE, BELOW] The new Burlington Northern operated its own passenger trains for only fourteen months, from March 2, 1970, through April 30, 1971. During that time little changed, except for the mixing of equipment and locomotives between the merger partners, production of Burlington Northern timetables, and some repainting of equipment. These scenes offer a taste of the short-lived Burlington Northern passenger era. Burlington Northern's version of Northern Pacific's *Mainstreeter* slows to a stop at the depot in Detroit Lakes in July 1970. While the locomotives still wear Northern Pacific paint, the train includes two ex–Great Northern cars, a sign of the intermixing of passenger equipment brought about by the merger. Next stop for the *Mainstreeter* will be Perham. Collection of Mark R. Lynn.

[RIGHT, ABOVE] The eastbound *Western Star* crosses the Sauk River west of Melrose in April 1971, a few days before service ended. Several cars have been repainted in Burlington Northern's green and white passenger train colors. The *Star*'s route west of Minneapolis shifted several times over the years. Its last move was in February 1970, from Great Northern's main line through Willmar to its route via St. Cloud and Fergus Falls. The *Star* was shifted to cover the territory served by the *Winnipeg Limited* and the St. Paul–Fargo *Dakotan,* which had used the St. Cloud line but were discontinued that same month. Photograph by George A. Forero Jr.

[RIGHT, BELOW] Except for the new numbers on the locomotive, there's little to tell this isn't a Great Northern train as Burlington Northern train 48 makes its station stop at the border town of Noyes on July 21, 1970. The train, which once ran on an overnight St. Paul–Winnipeg schedule, has been reduced to a Winnipeg–Grand Forks, North Dakota, day train. It connected with the *Western Star* in Grand Forks, which allowed passengers to travel to points east and west. Photograph by George A. Forero Jr.

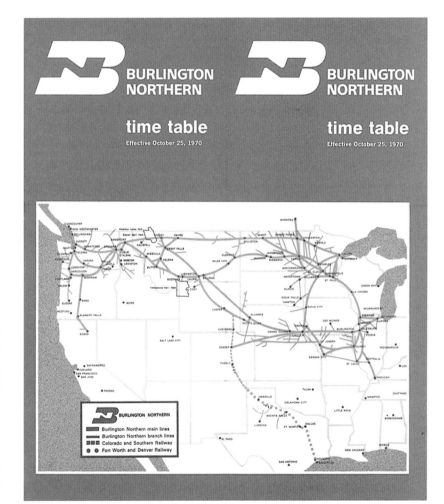

[OPPOSITE] In the final years of privately operated rail passenger service, railroads cut expenses wherever they could. Maintaining a depot was expensive, especially as service dwindled to one or two trains a day. Burlington Northern's depot at Crookston in 1971 was this tiny building, served by Grand Forks–Winnipeg trains 47 and 48. Train 47 is making its stop on April 17, 1971. It will make its last run in just thirteen days. Photograph by Baron Behning.

Burlington Northern's second, and last, public passenger train timetable was issued October 25, 1970. It was a meager fifteen pages, a far cry from the thick timetables issued by the railroads in the 1940s and 1950s. Author's collection.

[ABOVE] The date is April 30, 1971, and this is the last day for the St. Paul Union Depot. The depot switcher is shuffling cars while the power from the inbound *Empire Builder* waits on the right. The locomotives on the left will pull the combined *Empire Builder/Morning Zephyr/North Coast Limited* to Chicago. The last train out, train 9, the *Afternoon Zephyr* for Minneapolis, will depart close to midnight. The next day Amtrak's *Empire Builder* will bypass the building en route to the Great Northern Station in Minneapolis. Passenger trains are expected to return to the depot in 2012 after an absence of forty-one years. Photograph by Byron D. Olsen.

[OPPOSITE, ABOVE] If you bought a ticket at the St. Paul Union Depot in the 1950s or 1960s, it was issued with the logos of the eight railroads that served the building. A ninth, the Minneapolis & St. Louis, scaled back service to Minneapolis in the 1930s. Author's collection.

[OPPOSITE, BELOW] Inside the depot concourse in November 1970 are signs for the *North Coast Limited, Empire Builder,* and *Zephyr*. These were rolled in front of the departure gate and illuminated in order to direct passengers to the track their train would be departing from. Photograph by Byron D. Olsen.

OCTOBER 25, 1970

Passenger Train Schedules

THE MILWAUKEE ROAD

CHICAGO, MILWAUKEE, ST. PAUL AND PACIFIC RAILROAD

SUPER DOME

Hiawathas

CHICAGO
MILWAUKEE
ST. PAUL
MINNEAPOLIS

Western Cities Trains

CHICAGO
LOS ANGELES
SAN FRANCISCO
PORTLAND
DENVER

LINES ELECTRICALLY OPERATED 216 MILES

LINES ELECTRICALLY OPERATED 440 MILES

RAND McNALLY & CO.

[ABOVE] Milwaukee Road's last public timetable was only eight pages, showing seventeen trains. Issued on October 25, 1970, only three trains in the timetable reached the Twin Cities. Author's collection.

[LEFT] Like the St. Paul Union Depot, the Minneapolis Milwaukee Road Depot saw its last trains on April 30, 1971. By then the depot served only three trains: the eastbound and westbound *Morning Hiawathas* and the Minneapolis–Chicago *Fast Mail,* which had lost its U.S. mail contract and was reduced to only one or two coaches. When the *Morning Hiawatha* arrived in Minneapolis on April 30, its cars were immediately placed on that evening's *Fast Mail* to return the equipment to Chicago. The long train is rolling out of the depot, ending seventy-one years of Milwaukee Road passenger service at the station. Photograph by *Minneapolis Star Tribune,* Minnesota Historical Society Collection.

[OPPOSITE] Amtrak's Chicago–Seattle *Empire Builder* makes its first arrival at the Great Northern Station in Minneapolis on May 1, 1971. The train looks identical to the Burlington Northern version, but it used the Milwaukee Road route from Chicago to St. Paul via Milwaukee instead of the former Burlington Route through northern Illinois. The big difference at the depot was the number of trains. On April 30, it served eleven Burlington Northern trains, but beginning May 1 there would be only two Amtrak trains. Some Burlington Northern passenger trains that departed the West Coast on April 30 took over a day to reach Minneapolis; they finished their runs on May 2. Photograph by *Minneapolis Star Tribune,* Minnesota Historical Society Collection.

EFFECTIVE NOVEMBER 14, 1971

NATIONWIDE
SCHEDULES OF
INTERCITY
PASSENGER
SERVICE

National Railroad Passenger Corporation.
955 L'Enfant Plaza North, S.W., Washington, D.C. 20024

[LEFT] Amtrak issued a timetable on start-up day, May 1, 1971, but it was a hastily assembled document that was a rehash of private railroad schedules. Amtrak's first true timetable was issued on November 14, 1971, and included new trains, quick reference schedules, and detailed nationwide schedules, unlike anything seen before in the rail industry.

[BELOW] In its first few years of existence, except for new paint, Amtrak trains were much the same as they had been under private operation. Amtrak's *Hiawatha* crosses the Stone Arch Bridge departing Minneapolis for Chicago in September 1973. The motive power includes two former Milwaukee Road diesels painted in Amtrak's red and silver colors. The Minneapolis skyline is much changed since this photograph was taken. To the right of the diesels is the new Federal Reserve Bank on Marquette Avenue. This building would be replaced in 1997 with a structure built on the site of the Great Northern Station where this train originated. Photograph by Steve Glischinski.

Bound for Chicago, the *North Coast Hiawatha*'s diesels pour smoke as they pass Oakland Tower in St. Paul on March 21, 1976. The tower controlled the junction with the Milwaukee Road's Pig's Eye Yard, Burlington Northern's Dayton's Bluff Yard, and the joint Burlington Northern–Milwaukee Road main line. Amtrak 406 is right at home on this train—it was built for the Milwaukee Road in 1956 and pulled Milwaukee *Hiawatha*s over this track. The rods in the foreground lead from levers in the tower to switches and allow the operator to throw the switches from inside the tower. Photograph by Chuck Lavallee.

New locomotives had arrived when the *Empire Builder* passed the depot at Wayzata at sunrise on June 20, 1976. The locomotives are the 3,000-horsepower SDP40F models developed for Amtrak. The former Great Northern Wayzata depot opened in 1906 and is listed on the National Register of Historic Places. It is home to the Wayzata Historical Society and the Greater Wayzata Area Chamber of Commerce. The *Empire Builder* continued to pass the Wayzata depot until October 1979, when it was shifted to the route through St. Cloud when Amtrak discontinued the *North Coast Hiawatha* because of funding cuts. Photograph by Steve Glischinski.

A new Amtrak paint design was in use by the time of this photograph of Amtrak's *Empire Builder* at the Great Northern Station in Minneapolis on November 28, 1977. The maintenance crew is shoveling out a switch before the long train rolls to Willmar, Breckenridge, and points west. The station will close in only in three months. Photograph by Steve Glischinski.

[ABOVE] On its last night, February 28, 1978, the waiting room of the Great Northern Station in Minneapolis is nearly empty. The building opened in 1914 and had been open continuously since, but the next morning Amtrak's westbound *Empire Builder* would depart and the station would close. A new Amtrak station in St. Paul's Midway area replaced it. That summer the Great Northern Station was demolished. Photograph by Steve Glischinski.

[OPPOSITE] Northern Pacific's Como repair shops opened in St. Paul in 1886 and were tasked with servicing and maintaining Northern Pacific's fleet of passenger cars. Work flagged as passenger service waned, but Amtrak contracted with the shops to rebuild its cars in the early 1970s, where a shop worker is engaged in making repairs to an Amtrak car. After the Amtrak work was completed, Como Shops switched to maintenance of Burlington Northern's fleet of private business cars and cabooses until it closed in 1982. The City of St. Paul bought the shops and transformed them into the Bandana Square office and retail complex in 1983 and 1984. Photograph by Joe Elliott; collection of Aaron Isaacs.

The 1970s were tough times for many railroads, but the conservatively managed Soo Line remained profitable. The Soo believed in squeezing its assets to get as much return on investment as possible. The evidence can be seen at Gully on August 20, 1970, where wooden caboose 161 brings up the rear of train 73. Soo didn't purchase a new steel caboose until 1966 and wouldn't replace the last of its wooden cabooses, some of which dated to the 1880s, until 1973 and 1974. Five wooden cars held on in switching service as late as the early 1980s. Photograph by George A. Forero Jr.

A good source of traffic for railroads in the northern part of the state was pulpwood. Logs were trucked to sidings for loading into gondolas that the railroads would move to paper mills. Generally the hauls were short and just a few cars at a time. After deregulation of railroads in 1980, larger companies moved away from this type of "loose car" traffic, tending toward more cost-effective unit trains. Except for some regional and short lines, pulpwood traffic largely dried up. In March 1973 there was plenty of business for Soo train 72 at Palisade, with a large pile of logs across from the depot and several gondolas behind the locomotive. Photograph by George A. Forero Jr.

[ABOVE] Not as well known as the Mesabi Iron Range, the Cuyuna Iron Range is largely within Crow Wing County, roughly on a line between Brainerd and Aitkin. The Cuyuna was served first by the Soo Line in 1911, followed by the Northern Pacific in 1913. Both railroads had ore docks in Superior, Wisconsin. In 1929, the two companies signed an ore traffic pooling agreement, which provided for the common use of facilities and equipment between Superior and Ironton, Minnesota. The Soo began using Northern Pacific's Superior ore dock and tracks between McGregor and Ironton. In March 1973 a trainload of Cuyuna ore heads east for Superior on the Soo Line near Lawler. The photographer is perched in a fire tower to capture this image. Photograph by George A. Forero Jr.

[OPPOSITE, ABOVE] The McGregor depot agent is outside looking over Burlington Northern train 158, a freight headed from Staples to Superior, Wisconsin, as it bangs over the crossing with the Soo Line on February 11, 1978. Photograph by Steve Glischinski.

[OPPOSITE, BELOW] It's July 4, 1973, and the arrivals and departures board in the joint Burlington Northern–Soo Line depot in McGregor tells the story—all the passenger trains have been discontinued, leaving the agent with no tickets to sell. The two-story McGregor depot originally served only the Soo, but in 1929 it was moved several blocks to the crossing of the two railroads, replacing an interlocking tower and the Northern Pacific depot. Photograph by George A. Forero Jr.

[ABOVE, LEFT] By 1980, only one Cuyuna Range mine remained in operation, and rail movements were few and far between. It's hard to even make out the rails in this scene at Ironton on July 28, 1981, as a Soo Line train uses a runaround track through the weeds to get to the head end of the train. By this time most Soo ore cars had been retired, and the railroad borrowed cars from the Duluth, Missabe & Iron Range. The last Soo trains out of the Cuyuna were operated out of the Virginia Mine in the fall of 1984. Photograph by Tom Carlson.

The first major railroad restoration project for the Minnesota Transportation Museum was rebuilding Dan Patch Lines 100. This historic locomotive was built in 1913 by General Electric and was among the first successful internal combustion locomotives. In 1978, the museum rebuilt and repainted No. 100 in its original Dan Patch Line colors. No. 100 greets the sunrise at Burlington Northern's Como Shops on February 25, 1978. Later that day it moved under its own power to the General Electric Apparatus Shop in Minneapolis, which assisted in rebuilding the locomotive's trucks (the parts that support the car body and wheels). Photograph by Steve Glischinski.

Dan Patch Lines sold No. 100 to the Central Warehouse Company of St. Paul in 1917, which converted it to electric operation. No. 100 was sold in 1922 to the Minneapolis, Anoka and Cuyuna Range, an interurban electric railroad between Minneapolis and Anoka. In 1943 Northern Pump Company of Minneapolis built the Northern Ordnance Plant in Fridley, purchased the railroad, and rebuilt the line to move workers to the plant. The line from Fridley to Anoka was abandoned, but freight service was provided to the plant and the City of Minneapolis Water Department. In 1957, No. 100 received a 250-horsepower diesel engine and the overhead electric wire was removed. Great Northern purchased the Minneapolis, Anoka & Cuyuna Range in December 1966 and donated No. 100 to the Minnesota Transportation Museum in 1967. It is pulling freight in Fridley in March 1964. Photograph by *Minneapolis Star Tribune*, Minnesota Historical Society Collection.

The Duluth Union Depot was opened in 1892. It was saved from destruction in 1971 and preserved as the St. Louis County Heritage & Arts Center. In 1973 the Lake Superior Museum of Transportation & Industry was incorporated to open a railroad museum on the site, and a train shed was built over six of the old arrival/departure tracks to house displays and equipment. The museum's name was formally changed to Lake Superior Railroad Museum on December 1, 1997. The depot building, with the shed housing the railroad museum visible to the right, is seen on May 10, 1975. Photograph by Steve Glischinski.

Duluth, Missabe & Iron Range vice president and general manager Donald B. Shank invited executives of railroads and companies that did business with them to join the Lake Superior Railroad Museum's board of directors. They were able to secure the donation of equipment and often restored it prior to donation. This was the case with Duluth & Northeastern 28, which the railroad restored before donating it to the museum in 1974. Museum members are inspecting No. 28 as Burlington Northern moves it into the museum. The locomotive was built in 1906 for the Duluth, Missabe & Northern and sold to Duluth & Northeastern in 1955. Collection of Lake Superior Railroad Museum.

The last trains to use the Duluth Union Depot were Northern Pacific rail diesel cars to Staples. On the morning of May 24, 1969, train 58 arrived in Duluth from Staples, and when train 57 departed that evening, privately operated rail passenger service to Duluth ended. The depot was acquired in 1971 by the Area Cultural Corporation and turned over to St. Louis County. In April 1970 the waiting room of the empty depot appears suspended in time, waiting for trains that will never return. The false ceiling, installed in 1945, was removed during restoration. This area is now the Great Hall and used for large gatherings and special events. Photograph by Lyman Nylander; courtesy of the Northeast Minnesota Historical Center, Duluth (photograph S2420, b1f1).

[ABOVE, LEFT] Railroads in Minnesota frequently find themselves in a battle against Old Man Winter to keep their lines open for traffic. On March 28, 1975, an eastbound Soo Line snowplow extra blasts through a snow-filled cut near Barrett. This was one of three snowplow trains the railroad operated that day to Glenwood from Minneapolis, Thief River Falls, and this one from Enderlin, North Dakota. Photograph by Steve Glischinski.

[ABOVE, RIGHT] Crossing a desolate winter landscape, a local freight is pushing a plow west on the Soo's Brooten Line near Greenwald on February 1, 1975. The Soo Line constructed the Brooten Line in 1914 to serve as a cutoff between western Minnesota and Superior, Wisconsin. Photograph by Steve Glischinski.

[OPPOSITE] Life on the railroad is never easy, as photographer Forero, a manager for the Soo Line, found out while working to open the line between Minneapolis and Glenwood in early 1975. This snowplow is stopped at the Paynesville depot waiting for a new crew on January 12. He recalls: "We waited a couple of hours for the agent from Glenwood to drive out a replacement crew. The plow was opening the line as it went, so it was shut down (for about twenty-four hours) until it could reach Glenwood. Upon our arrival at Glenwood, an eastbound train was waiting to go, and I hopped on that. Unfortunately, just outside Buffalo the train derailed, and the line was tied up for another twelve hours or so until we got that cleaned up." Photograph by George A. Forero Jr.

The Brooten Line cut a swath across central Minnesota but served only small towns and had little on-line traffic. While it was an efficient route for grain traffic from the Dakotas to the Twin Ports, in the 1980s the Soo decided the two-hundred-mile line was too expensive to keep and rerouted traffic via the Twin Cities to Superior. The last remnant of the Brooten Line was pulled up in 1990. In better days, train 71 passes the depot at Holdingford on July 16, 1978. Photograph by Steve Glischinski.

Minnesota residents like to boast about how they can withstand the often brutal winters. Railroads have to contend with the same weather, and although passenger trains were often delayed by bad weather, they usually made it through. A case in point is this westbound Milwaukee Road passenger train at Winona. The ice-encased locomotives have been brought over to the depot, where a hose is being used to fill their steam boilers for train heat. It may be late, but this train will make it through to Minneapolis. Collection of John C. Luecke.

[OPPOSITE] In January 1970, the Milwaukee Road dropped its *Afternoon Hiawatha* service between Chicago and the Twin Cities, leaving the *Morning Hiawatha* as the last survivor of a fleet of *Hiawatha* streamliners that once reached from Chicago to the Pacific Northwest. The *Morning Hiawatha* remained a quality train, including a full-length Super Dome and a parlor car, although it lost its unique glass-enclosed Skytop observation car in April 1969. On May 3, 1970, the westbound streamliner makes its station stop in Winona. It would roll its last miles on April 30, 1971. Photograph by Baron Behning.

[ABOVE] The Milwaukee Road tracks through Winona bisected the city and were practically at the doorsteps of some homes. A westbound freight behind Milwaukee Road 96C, which once was assigned to pull passenger trains, is heading through a residential neighborhood in Winona on May 29, 1976. Notice that some panels on the twenty-five-year-old locomotive have been haphazardly replaced and now spell out "The Milwaukeee Rod." Photograph by George A. Forero Jr.

[LEFT] The 1970s were the last decade to see agents and operators working in depots, as technology would soon make their presence unnecessary. The depot at Red Wing was one of the few where the agent handled not only freight but Amtrak passenger trains as well. On August 24, 1975, the Red Wing agent waves to the caboose of a westbound Milwaukee Road freight. Agents were responsible for typing out orders for trains issued by dispatchers, preparing waybills for freight trains, keeping track of any cars in the local yard, communicating with the public, inspecting trains as they passed, and other duties as the railroads outlined them. Photograph by George A. Forero Jr.

[OPPOSITE] Milwaukee Road train 57, the *Fast Mail,* has fought heavy snow on its overnight run from Chicago as evidenced by the snow-caked diesel units under the shed at the Milwaukee Road Depot in Minneapolis in early 1971. The trains were operated primarily for hauling mail and express. The eastbound train (to Chicago) was 56, the westbound 57. The *Fast Mail* lost its mail contract in September 1970, and train 57 made its last run on March 28, 1971. Coach-only train 56 was the last train to depart Milwaukee's Minneapolis depot on the evening of April 30, 1971. Collection of John C. Luecke.

[ABOVE] After the snow melts, flooding can become a problem for railroads. April 1969 saw flooding of the Mississippi River in St. Paul and downstream. The Milwaukee Road's main line to Chicago followed the river between St. Paul and La Crosse, Wisconsin; with the river at flood stage, the railroad was forced to move its trains over other railroads. Some detoured over the Soo Line, creating the unusual sight of an eastbound Milwaukee Road streamliner crossing the Soo's St. Croix River Bridge between Minnesota and Wisconsin north of Stillwater. The flood crest at St. Paul was 25 feet on April 15, 1969, second only to the flood of 1965 at 26.4 feet. Photograph by Frank E. Sandberg Jr.

[ABOVE] Passenger trains weren't the only ones to encounter winter's fury. On February 16, 1976, a Milwaukee Road local is entering Preston in a snowstorm. After performing switching chores the train will head east to Caledonia. The Preston–Caledonia line began life as a three-foot-gauge line and was converted to standard gauge in 1901. The branch had lightweight track and bridges that could not support heavy diesels. Milwaukee Road's answer was to lash together three or four of its six-hundred-horsepower SW1 switch engines as seen here. At one hundred tons each, they were twenty to twenty-five tons lighter than most EMD switch engines. Photograph by Steve Glischinski.

[OPPOSITE, ABOVE] As highways were improved during the 1920s and after, trucks were able to reach more areas, which cut into railroads' market share. This spelled the end for branch lines, which were pulled up at an accelerated rate in the 1970s and 1980s. The Milwaukee Road's lines to Preston and the twenty-six-mile branch from Hastings to Stillwater were victims. The railroad abandoned the line from Hastings to Lakeland in 1979 in favor of operating rights over the Chicago & North Western. In March 1975 a short train rumbles through the snow at Lakeland heading back to Hastings. Photograph by George A. Forero Jr.

[OPPOSITE, BELOW] Four months later it's considerably warmer in Bayport as the local train has arrived from Hastings and stopped at the depot. The crew is looking over their paperwork to determine the day's switching moves on July 25, 1975. Photograph by Steve Glischinski.

[ABOVE] On September 8, 1977, Milwaukee Road's local from Farmington to Shakopee is about to pass under Interstate 35 at Lakeville. This route was abandoned in 1980 when the Milwaukee Road gained rights over Chicago & North Western tracks to reach Shakopee. Photograph by Steve Glischinski.

[LEFT] What a difference a few years can make! The same scene in May 2011 reveals little evidence that a railroad ever existed at this location. Only the bike path marks the location of the old railroad right of way. The tracks, and the Milwaukee Road itself, are long gone. Photograph by Jerry Huddleston.

The Milwaukee Road's original route from St. Paul to Minneapolis took it through Mendota, Fort Snelling, and Minnehaha Park. Just five miles south of the Milwaukee's Minneapolis depot is the Minnehaha depot, built in 1875. Dubbed the "Princess" it hosted excursion trains with travelers coming to the park to enjoy the beauty of the falls. In 1957 the line was cut at Mendota, and the track by the depot was seldom used. In February 1975 a switch job working the elevators along Hiawatha Avenue is moving past the depot to the Minnehaha siding, where it will run around its cars and head back north. The depot is now a museum. Photograph by Steve Glischinski.

[LEFT] Even though Amtrak took over most privately operated passenger service in the United States, there was still a non-Amtrak train in Minnesota in the 1970s. Canadian National Railways operated passenger service using rail diesel cars between Winnipeg and Thunder Bay, Ontario. Canadian National's route dipped south of Lake of the Woods, entering Minnesota at Warroad and heading back into Canada at Baudette. The rail diesel car made stops in Minnesota at both cities. Train 686 from Winnipeg is tucked into the siding by the Warroad depot as an eastbound passes by on December 14, 1974. Photograph by George A. Forero Jr.

[BELOW] On a summer day in July 1977, the baggage man on train 686 looks hopefully for passengers at the Baudette depot. The unique international passenger service ended later that year. Photograph by Steve Glischinski.

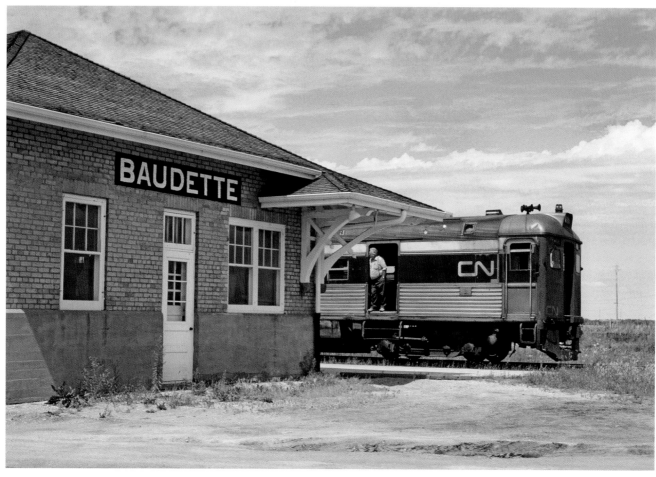

The crew of a Milwaukee Road freight from St. Paul pauses for a chat with the crew that will take the train to Aberdeen, South Dakota, on a snowy day in Montevideo in January 1973. Eventually the train will make its way to the Pacific Northwest over Milwaukee's Pacific Extension. Changes are on the horizon: Milwaukee Road would enter bankruptcy in 1977; the Pacific Extension would be abandoned west of Miles City, Montana, in 1980; and this portion of the railroad would be purchased by the Twin Cities & Western in 1991. The Montevideo depot is now a museum. Photograph by George A. Forero Jr.

[OPPOSITE, ABOVE] The interior of the Milwaukee Road depot at Cologne is immaculate as the operator uses his headset to talk with the dispatcher's office in July 1972. Photograph by Joe Elliott; collection of Aaron Isaacs.

[OPPOSITE, BELOW] Outside the depot an old boxcar bakes in the summer sun. Photograph by Joe Elliott; collection of Aaron Isaacs.

[ABOVE] A 1968 Mercury Cougar waits at the crossing in Hopkins as a Chicago & North Western local train rolls into town on June 9, 1973. The train is completing a journey over the former Minneapolis & St. Louis Railway line from Morton. Due to slow track conditions, the round trip from Minneapolis to Morton could take several days. Just about everything in this scene has changed: the line from Norwood to Hopkins was abandoned in 1980, the ex–Great Northern branch the lead locomotive is crossing has been pulled up, and the Cougar is now a collector's car. Even the three-screen Hopkins Theatre, visible on the right side of the photograph, is gone. Photograph by Baron Behning.

[LEFT, ABOVE] Meets between trains are common in railroading, but branch line meets are rare, since these lines usually warrant only a single train a day. The former Chicago Great Western branch between Red Wing and Cannon Falls proved the exception on October 28, 1972, when the Milwaukee Road local from Hastings met its Chicago & North Western counterpart from Red Wing. The Milwaukee crew had finished their work and pulled into a siding at Cannon Falls to clear. Engineer Dick Thompson prepares to give the North Western train a roll-by inspection. Milwaukee Road had rights over the line dating back to 1937 when they abandoned their own parallel branch. Photograph by Chuck Lavallee.

[LEFT, BELOW] Earlier in the day, the Milwaukee train headed west on a grass-covered right-of-way. Approaching the Highway 61 overpass near Red Wing, it encountered a cow that refused to yield the right-of-way until the last minute. Today this is part of the Cannon Valley Trail, which attracts nearly one hundred thousand users annually. Photograph by Chuck Lavallee.

[OPPOSITE, ABOVE] Chicago & North Western's network of branch lines in southern Minnesota was hopelessly unprofitable by the 1970s. Truck competition and years of deferred maintenance caught up with them, and the railroad aggressively pursued abandonments. On March 23, 1977, a local from Tracy is setting out its train of forty-foot boxcars at Morgan on the branch from Sleepy Eye to Redwood Falls. The engine and caboose will run to Redwood Falls and return to Tracy the next day. The twenty-five-mile line was abandoned later that year. Photograph by Steve Glischinski.

[OPPOSITE, BELOW] The sad state of business on secondary and branch lines in the 1970s is illustrated by this Chicago & North Western local creeping through the fog south of Hayfield on December 14, 1977. Less than a decade earlier this had been a portion of Chicago Great Western's main line from Hayfield to Austin, Mason City, and Omaha, but Chicago & North Western pulled up the portion from Austin to Waltham earlier in 1977, ending through service, and this train is bringing but a single car picked up at Waltham. Photograph by Steve Glischinski.

[ABOVE] On the former main line of the Chicago Great Western at Dodge Center, a northbound train from Oelwein, Iowa, crosses the Chicago & North Western line (Winona to Rapid City, South Dakota) in 1974. A westbound train from Winona waits in the distance. The locomotives on the northbound are EMD F-units, a favorite of railroad enthusiasts for their streamlined appearance. Photograph by Roger W. Bee.

[OPPOSITE] In northern Minnesota, steel companies used railroads to transport iron ore from their vast open pit mines to unloading facilities. One of the larger operations was Oliver Iron Mining, a part of US Steel Corporation. In mining areas large shovels were used to load cars, and tracks were moved as mining areas changed. On August 3, 1974, an Oliver train is pushing cars into the crusher at the Rouchleau Mine in Virginia. The locomotives, built by Baldwin, were referred to as cow and calf sets—the "cow" is equipped with a cab; a "calf" is not. Oliver's were the only cow and calf sets constructed by Baldwin. Photograph by Steve Glischinski.

[OPPOSITE] In rocky areas prone to slides, railroads installed slide detector fences. If a sizable rock touched or broke through a fence, the train would receive a red signal, and an indicator would light up at the dispatcher's or controlling office. One such installation was along the Mississippi River west of St. Croix Tower in Hastings, where an eastbound Burlington Northern freight winds along the rocky cliffs protected by the fences on June 23, 1974. Photograph by George A. Forero Jr.

[RIGHT, ABOVE] Each year the Rock Island handled the Royal American Shows train from the Minnesota State Fair to its next engagement in Kansas. The train at one time had ninety cars and moved in two sections. Royal American Shows switched to trucks in 1982 and played its last dates in 1997. On September 3, 1974, the train is crossing the Mississippi River at Inver Grove Heights. This area was the city of Inver Grove from 1909 until 1965 when it was merged into Inver Grove Heights. The Rock Island always referred to the area, which contained their classification yard, as Inver Grove. The bridge, built in 1895, was one of the few double-deck bridges on the Mississippi; the top level was for railroad traffic and the bottom for automobiles. It closed to rail traffic in 1980 and to road traffic in 1999. Photograph by Steve Glischinski.

[RIGHT, BELOW] The Rock Island declared bankruptcy for the final time in March 1975. In an effort to rehabilitate its image, it adopted a new blue and white paint scheme. Contrasting with the old maroon colors, a Soo Line transfer operating with Rock Island power crosses the Robert Street Lift Bridge in downtown St. Paul on April 22, 1978. The unpowered slug unit between the locomotives was touted as an energy saver, since it has trucks (wheels) with traction motors that help supply higher tractive effort to the locomotive but it does not contain a fuel-consuming engine. Photograph by Steve Glischinski.

American Locomotive (Alco) ceased production in 1969, and as railroads retired their Alco fleets, interest in them grew. Chicago & North Western ran a number of Alco diesel locomotives on the line between Winona, Mankato, and Tracy, which led to North Western's route being dubbed the "Alco Line" by railroad fans. In August 1975, at the height of the Alco craze, train 482 is making the scenic climb out of the Minnesota River Valley just east of Mankato behind four Alcos. Photograph by George A. Forero Jr.

[ABOVE] The *American Freedom Train* toured the forty-eight contiguous states in 1975 and 1976 to commemorate the U.S. Bicentennial. The twenty-six-car train was steam powered and marked the first time a main line steam locomotive operated in the state since the Burlington Route excursions of the early 1960s. In the train's ten display cars were over five hundred artifacts, including George Washington's copy of the Constitution, the original Louisiana Purchase, and a moon rock. Over a twenty-one-month period more than seven million Americans visited the train. It arrived in Minneapolis on August 25, 1975, and was displayed at Minnehaha Park, where visitors are waiting to tour it on August 28. A moving sidewalk whisked visitors past displays. Photograph by Baron Behning.

[RIGHT, ABOVE] The *Freedom Train*'s next stop after Minneapolis was Fargo, North Dakota. Pulled by former Southern Pacific 4-8-4 No. 4449, built in 1941 to pull the famous *Daylight* streamliners between Los Angeles and San Francisco, the train heads west across the Stone Arch Bridge in Minneapolis on August 31, 1975. Photograph by Steve Glischinski.

[RIGHT, BELOW] After the bicentennial celebration ended, 4449 embarked on a new career pulling excursion trains throughout the continental United States. Based in Portland, Oregon, a volunteer group maintains it. No. 4449 returned to Minnesota in the summer of 2009 when it passed through en route to a railroad fair in Michigan, and it returned for a weekend of excursions for the nonprofit Friends of the 261 in October. Clad in its original Southern Pacific *Daylight* colors, 4449 is making time on Canadian Pacific's former Milwaukee Road Mississippi River Line on August 3, 2009. This is the same route it traveled with the *Freedom Train* thirty-four years earlier. Photograph by Steve Glischinski.

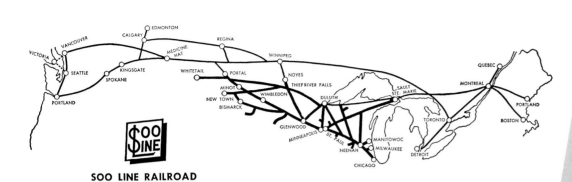

SOO LINE RAILROAD

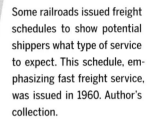

FAST FREIGHT SCHEDULES

between
Points on Soo Line
and
CONNECTIONS

F. R. CROW
Freight Service Manager
Minneapolis, Minn.
Issued February 1, 1960

[OPPOSITE, ABOVE] The United States has seen two national *Freedom Train* tours. The original *American Freedom Train* traveled the United States from September 1947 to January 1949. Guarded by a contingent of U.S. Marines, the seven-car train carried original versions of the Constitution, Declaration of Independence, and the Bill of Rights on a tour of more than three hundred cities in all forty-eight states. Minnesota stops were made at Brainerd, Duluth, Minneapolis, St. Cloud, St. Paul, and Willmar in early May 1948. In this view, the train is on display at the rail spur across Como Avenue from the Minnesota State Fairgrounds in St. Paul. Photograph by Ronald V. Nixon, Museum of the Rockies Photo Archive.

[OPPOSITE, BELOW] With the abandonment of passenger service, the small town railroad depot lost one of the main reasons for its existence. However, depots still functioned as the railroads' operating offices. They were staffed by operators who were in communication with dispatchers. The dispatchers issued train orders to notify trains of meets and other operating conditions. The Soo Line depot at Withrow sat at the junction with the main line to Chicago and the line to Duluth and Sault Ste. Marie. It was open twenty-four hours a day. On a chilly winter night in 1973, the lonely depot is a beacon of light in an otherwise dark landscape. Photograph by John Cartwright.

[RIGHT] Twelve miles west of Withrow at Cardigan Junction in Shoreview, the operator works the night shift taking down train orders. He will use a special hoop to hand them up to trains as they pass by. In the 1980s railroads began using radios to issue orders directly to crews in the locomotive, rendering depots and their operators superfluous. Photograph by Joe Elliott; collection of Aaron Isaacs.

Some railroads issued freight schedules to show potential shippers what type of service to expect. This schedule, emphasizing fast freight service, was issued in 1960. Author's collection.

[ABOVE] Toward the end of the era of depots and their agents, Soo Line train 942 from Thief River Falls meets a northbound by the Detroit Lakes depot in November 1977. The Soo was known for well-maintained equipment and clean diesels such as these. Photograph by Tom Carlson.

[OPPOSITE, ABOVE] The longest and highest railroad bridge in Minnesota crosses the St. Croix River on the Minnesota–Wisconsin border west of Somerset, Wisconsin. Completed in 1911 by the Wisconsin Central Railroad, the steel bridge is 2,682 feet long and 184 feet high. Wisconsin Central was one of three railroads that merged to form the new Soo Line Railroad Company in 1961. On October 2, 1976, Soo train 944 crosses the massive structure heading east. The bridge was added to the National Register of Historic Places on August 22, 1977. Photograph by Steve Glischinski.

[OPPOSITE, BELOW] On January 19, 1975, photographer Forero, a licensed pilot, flew over the St. Croix River Bridge to capture this view of train 944 heading east with four diesels. In 1987, the Soo sold most of its Badger State lines to a new regional, also named Wisconsin Central, which included the St. Croix Bridge. In 2012 it belongs to Canadian National, which acquired Wisconsin Central in 2001. Photograph by George A. Forero Jr.

[OPPOSITE] The Soo Line had two other bridges that crossed the St. Croix River on the Minnesota–Wisconsin border, near Osceola and at Danbury, Wisconsin. The Danbury Bridge was on Soo's Duluth–St. Paul line. This route was mainly in Wisconsin but cut through a wilderness area of Minnesota east of Hinckley. The Danbury Bridge was seldom photographed because of the relatively isolated area and because trains were likely to run at night. The author was lucky when southbound train 77 from Superior ran late on March 31, 1979, and crossed the bridge from Minnesota into Wisconsin in daylight. Photograph by Steve Glischinski.

[ABOVE] Burlington Northern's five-day-a-week local is rumbling over the wood trestle at Orono on the Hutchinson Branch in November 1975. In the 1980s, this branch would be a microcosm of the changes coming to the railroad industry in Minnesota: it would be turned over to short line Dakota Rail in 1985, see passenger dinner trains from 1986 to 1989, and be abandoned in 2001. Photograph by Steve Glischinski.

[ABOVE] The shutdown of the Chicago, Rock Island & Pacific in 1980 had a dramatic effect on southern Minnesota railroading. Chicago & North Western gained control of the Rock's main line from the Twin Cities into Iowa, then tore up the entire ex–Chicago Great Western main line in Minnesota. It also abandoned portions of the former Minneapolis & St. Louis that paralleled the Rock Island to the west. Where once there were three main line railroads, only one remained. The last northbound Rock Island train from Manly, Iowa, to Inver Grove Heights passes the depot at Farmington on March 30, 1980. The next day the Rock Island shut down forever. Photograph by Steve Glischinski.

[LEFT] Railroads issued timetables for the use of employees, but they were unlike passenger timetables used by the public. These documents spelled out all the stations, sidings, speed restrictions, signaling systems and other information necessary for employees to safely operate trains over a section of track. There were often dozens of these timetables issued for different areas or divisions of the railroad, but in later years many lines consolidated their employee timetables into one large booklet. This is the first and only system employee timetable issued by the Rock Island in 1979. Author's collection.

3

Revival and Rehabilitation

1980–2000

WITH THE SHUTDOWN OF THE ROCK ISLAND and the embargo of much of the Milwaukee Road in early 1980, the first year of the new decade didn't look much different from the year before. However, on October 14, 1980, President Jimmy Carter signed landmark legislation that partially deregulated the railroad industry. Named for Representative Harley O. Staggers of West Virginia, the Staggers Rail Act is largely responsible for the industry's health in the twenty-first century.

The effects of the Staggers Act were far-reaching. The abandonment process was accelerated and streamlined so that railroads were finally able to shed thousands of miles of underused lines. Railroads were free to set rates and enter into contracts with shippers to set price and service without the interference of the Interstate Commerce Commission. Merger proceedings were streamlined and time limits were set to prevent a recurrence of the Rock

Island–Union Pacific merger debacle. The Interstate Commerce Commission itself disappeared in 1995, replaced by the smaller Federal Surface Transportation Board.[1]

As deregulation took hold, there were more changes to the Minnesota railroad scene. One was the departure of Burlington Northern's headquarters from St. Paul. Hints of a move came as early as 1978, when Burlington Northern began a study to determine the practicality of moving out of Minnesota, known at the time for higher-than-average corporate and personal income taxes. The tax situation was galling to Burlington Northern chairman Louis W. Menk, who had long been a critic of Minnesota's business climate and met several times with Minnesota's governor about the situation.[2]

Burlington Northern didn't make a big announcement before pulling out of the state. It did so slowly and quietly. In 1981, Burlington Northern's large holding company departed for Seattle, and in 1983 the operating department went to Kansas City. The next year the marketing and coal departments moved to Fort Worth, Texas. By January 1, 1985, the general offices of the company were officially listed as being in Fort Worth.[3]

Because of deregulation, Burlington Northern was able to abandon approximately 649 miles of line in Minnesota between 1980 and 1990. It also sold or leased other secondary and branch lines, another process made easier with deregulation. In 1984 the railroad announced its intention to abandon its Wayzata–Hutchinson branch, but instead the line was sold to Dakota Rail Inc., which began operating it in December 1985.[4]

There were more spin-offs of branch and secondary lines. On October 27, 1986, the Otter Tail Valley Railroad commenced service over 151 miles of track between Avon and Moorhead, plus short branches out of Fergus Falls, the line's headquarters. Burlington Northern also sold 667 miles of track, mainly in North Dakota, to the Red River Valley & Western in 1987. Its shop and dispatching offices are in Breckenridge.[5]

Midsized regional railroads popped up in the 1980s and 1990s because of two major factors. One was the bankruptcy of the Rock Island and Milwaukee Road. Several smaller carriers, such as I&M Rail Link (later Iowa, Chicago & Eastern) and Twin Cities & Western, rose from the ashes of these bankrupt systems. The other factor was that the sale of marginal routes by larger railroads was made easier by deregulation. Regional railroads were able to operate these routes more efficiently and provide personalized service, since the new start-ups were not hampered by the antiquated work rules of the bigger railroads (rules that are largely gone today) and local management could concentrate on service.[6]

The largest regional railroad in Minnesota was the Dakota, Minnesota & Eastern. It began operations on September 5, 1986, over track sold by the Chicago & North Western. Dakota, Minnesota & Eastern eventually operated a 1,105-mile system, including 316 miles of track and trackage rights in Minnesota. Its main line extended from Winona across southern Minnesota through Waseca, Mankato, and Tracy to Rapid City, South Dakota.[7]

In 1997, Dakota, Minnesota & Eastern announced a proposal to expand the railroad into Wyoming to reach huge deposits of low-sulphur coal served by Burlington Northern and Union Pacific. More than 260 miles of new railroad were planned as well as upgrading the main line through Minnesota to handle unit coal trains at a cost of $1.4 billion.[8] However, the City of Rochester and the Mayo Clinic feared the long coal trains would disrupt sensitive instruments at the medical facility, even though it was several blocks away. There was enough opposition that the federal government denied the railroad a key loan to finance the expansion in 2007.[9] Canadian Pacific acquired Dakota, Minnesota & Eastern in 2008 and quietly shelved the coal plan.

The sale of the downsized Milwaukee Road to the Soo Line led to its demise and the birth of a new regional railroad. When traffic and income of the smaller Milwaukee Road began heading upward, three railroads vied to buy the company: Chicago & North Western; Michigan's Grand Trunk Corporation, parent of the Grand Trunk Western Railroad;

and the Soo Line. Grand Trunk had originally proposed acquiring the slimmed-down Milwaukee Road in 1981. In 1983, the Milwaukee Road's first profitable year since 1974, Chicago & North Western entered the contest, followed by the Soo Line in 1984. The bidding soon priced Grand Trunk out of the market, but the North Western and Soo continued the battle. The Chicago & North Western actually submitted a higher offer to the Milwaukee's bankruptcy court, but the judge overseeing the case, citing the North Western's intent to abandon hundreds of miles of line, awarded the railroad to the Soo, saying its bid was more in the public interest.[10]

Assuming that Chicago & North Western would win the bidding for the railroad, the Soo was caught unaware with no real integration plan for the merger. It began losing money as it attempted to absorb the Milwaukee Road into its system.[11] Looking for ways to return to profitability, it sold its original track in Wisconsin along with two former Milwaukee Road routes to the new Wisconsin Central Ltd. on October 11, 1987.[12] For the next fourteen years, Wisconsin Central was a railroad success story, concentrating on customer service, traffic growth, and expansion. The railroad served the Twin Cities using rights over Canadian Pacific track from Withrow to Minneapolis and also operated a branch from Withrow to Dresser and Amery, Wisconsin. The company was so successful that Canadian National purchased it in 2001 and integrated it into its expanding U.S. network.

The Soo Line suffered the same fate as eventually befell Wisconsin Central: integration into a larger Canadian railroad. After buying the Milwaukee Road, the Soo had three years of heavy losses until finally finding profitability again in 1988. Majority owner Canadian Pacific attempted to sell its interest in the company but abandoned its search to find a buyer in March 1989. Instead, it purchased the 44 percent of the Soo it did not already own at a cost of $21.50 a share.[13] The purchase was completed in January 1990. Canadian Pacific took a slow approach to integrating its old subsidiary, gradually phasing out the Soo Line name and colors, so that many Soo locomotives remained in their old paint into the twenty-first century.

One of the reasons the Soo Line lost money after buying the Milwaukee Road was the deteriorated state of its physical plant. Although the Milwaukee Road had been making an effort to catch up on deferred maintenance after it downsized, it wasn't up to Soo Line standards. In the 1960s and 1970s, this might have been allowed to continue due to a lack of capital. With railroads gaining more traffic and revenue in the 1980s and 1990s, the Soo Line in 1988 embarked on a five-year, $65-million improvement program for the Chicago–Twin Cities main line. The upgrade included new welded rail, reducing the double-track line down to one track, new sidings, ties, and new rock ballast for drainage. The old Milwaukee Road system of electrical relays and line side wires used for communication and signaling were removed in favor of a new computer-controlled signal system.[14]

Canadian Pacific sold off two major portions of the former Soo–Milwaukee Road system in the 1990s. Its former Milwaukee Road route west of the Twin Cities roughly paralleled that of the former Soo line and was an attractive candidate for sale since it had ample local business: approximately seventeen thousand carloads annually. Traffic included coal, grain, sugar, food products, fertilizer, and crushed rock.[15]

In 1991, Canadian Pacific put the line on the block, and the winning bid came from Oakes Development Corporation, which had formed the Red River Valley & Western Railroad in 1987. Oakes formed the Twin Cities & Western Railroad Company to operate the line. Twin Cities & Western and Red River Valley & Western operated as sister railroads, but each with its own management structure. The Twin Cities & Western began operations when the sale was consummated on July 26, 1991. The first revenue move was made on July 27, 1991, with official ribbon-cutting ceremonies held in Glencoe on August 4, 1991.[16]

When it began, Twin Cities & Western owned 143 miles of track, from just west of Hopkins to Appleton. Twin Cities & Western also gained rights over 33 miles of Canadian Pacific and Burlington Northern track from Appleton to Milbank, South Dakota, to connect with a short line railroad there. Twin Cities & Western is based in Glencoe and in 2002 added 94 miles of former Minneapolis & St. Louis track from Norwood to Hanley Falls. Subsidiary Minnesota Prairie Line operates this track.[17]

In 1997, Canadian Pacific sold its ex–Milwaukee Road secondary lines in southern Minnesota and its routes in Iowa; its Rockford, Illinois–Janesville, Wisconsin, branch line; and the Chicago–Kansas City main line to new start-up I&M Rail Link. Based in Davenport, Iowa, privately held I&M Rail Link had a tough go from its first day in April 1997, when floods closed its main line in the Quad Cities. It is believed the company never achieved profitability. In 2002, it sold out to Iowa, Chicago & Eastern.[18]

With deregulation railroads were freer than ever to merge, and the 1990s saw merger mania in the industry. Railroad corporate consolidations had been part of the U.S. railroad scene since soon after the first rails were laid, but the final movement toward the seven Class 1 systems of 2012 picked up steam in the early 1980s. (A Class 1 system is defined as having annual operating revenue exceeding $379 million as of 2009.) These seven systems account for approximately 67 percent of U.S. freight rail mileage, 89 percent of employees, and 93 percent of revenue.[19]

In Minnesota, the Class 1 railroad with the largest amount of track is the BNSF Railway. It was the result of the September 22, 1995, merger of Burlington Northern Inc. with the Santa Fe Pacific Corporation. Their two railroad subsidiaries, the Atchison, Topeka & Santa Fe Railway and Burlington Northern Railroad were merged on December 31, 1996.[20]

Burlington Northern was the result of the successful 1970 merger of the Burlington, Great Northern, Northern Pacific, and Spokane, Portland & Seattle railways.

Unlike Burlington Northern, Santa Fe was one of the most well-known railways; its name had remained virtually intact since 1863, with only a minor change from "railroad" to "railway" in December 1895. Famous for its fine passenger train service, in the 1980s and 1990s the Santa Fe remade itself as a high-speed intermodal railroad; its franchise line was the Chicago to Los Angeles main line, which once hosted several transcontinental streamliners.[21] Named the Burlington Northern and Santa Fe Railway in 1995, the name was changed to BNSF Railway in January

2005. In Minnesota the railroad operated 1,598 miles of track as of 2011.[22]

Among the oldest names in railroading is Union Pacific, which came to Minnesota in 1995 when it purchased Chicago & North Western. Union Pacific began as the eastern link of the first transcontinental railroad from Omaha, Nebraska, to Promontory, Utah, where it linked up with the Central Pacific on May 10, 1869. Union Pacific was known as a pioneer in railroading. In 1935, it introduced the nation's first streamliner, the M-10000. In 1941, Union Pacific received the first Big Boy, the largest steam locomotive ever built, and in 1969 it introduced the largest diesel locomotive ever built to that time, the 6,600-horsepower Centennial named for Union Pacific's one hundredth anniversary.[23]

Today's Union Pacific is the result of several mergers. It acquired the Western Pacific in 1981 and the Missouri Pacific in 1982, extending its system to San Francisco and throughout the south-central states. In 1988, it added the Missouri–Kansas–Texas ("Katy") that linked Kansas City with Houston and San Antonio. In 1995 Union Pacific acquired Chicago & North Western, and in 1996, Union Pacific merged with Southern Pacific Lines, expanding its system by over fourteen thousand miles. Included in the acquisition was Southern Pacific's Denver & Rio Grande Western. Based in Omaha, Union Pacific is the largest U.S. railroad, operating a thirty-two-thousand-mile network. Well aware of its history, Union Pacific operates two large steam locomotives as part of its Heritage Program, which also includes diesels and passenger cars used on streamliners in the 1950s.[24]

Union Pacific's presence in Minnesota comes from its purchase of Chicago & North Western. The North Western, Union Pacific, and Burlington Northern all were able to increase their revenues in the 1980s and 1990s thanks to the movement of western coal. In Minnesota, Chicago & North Western served Northern States Power coal-burning plants in Bayport and Burnsville, while Burlington Northern handled coal to several plants across the state. The railroads' successors, Union Pacific and BNSF Railway, continue to move coal to Minnesota and hundreds of other customers across the United States.

How important is coal to railroad revenues? In 2000, U.S. railroads moved approximately 27,763,000 total carloads, of which coal accounted for 6,954,000, or about 25 percent. Also in 2000, railroads generated approximately $36.331 billion of freight revenue, with coal contributing about $7.794 billion, or 21.5 percent of total revenue. The next-largest revenue generator for railroads, chemicals and allied products, accounted for only $4.68 billion in revenue and 1,860,000 carloads.[25] The three primary destinations for U.S. coal are coal-fired power plants, ports to export coal, and domestic facilities used to make coke, which is used in steel manufacturing.[26]

Another area of revenue growth for railroads has been intermodal—moving shipping containers or truck trailers on railcars with no handling of the freight when changing between modes. According to the Association of American Railroads, rail intermodal traffic has quadrupled since 1980. It rose from 3 million trailers and containers in 1980 to more than 12 million in 2006 and 2007. In 2008, intermodal accounted for 22 percent of rail revenue.[27]

REVIVAL AND REHABILITATION, 1980–2000

BNSF Railway maintains a large intermodal facility in the Midway area of St. Paul, and Canadian Pacific converted the former Soo Line Shoreham Yard in north Minneapolis into an intermodal terminal. Both railroads also run intermodal trains that pass through the state en route to other destinations. On BNSF, the hottest trains on the railroad are Z trains—intermodal trains that operate on tight schedules, much like passenger trains of the past.

In Minnesota, Union Pacific has not been a large intermodal carrier, but the trains it does run are unique. Beginning in 2004, Union Pacific began operating a roadrailer train from Minneapolis to Chicago. Roadrailers are truck trailers built with railroad wheel sets. After loading, a truck pulls the trailer to a rail yard, where the wheels are lowered into position on the tracks. Since no flatcars are involved, there is no need to have a crane system to transfer the trailer between modes. Union Pacific moves the trains for Triple Crown Services, a subsidiary of Norfolk Southern Railway. Triple Crown set up a roadrailer facility at Union Pacific's East Minneapolis Yard for the service, the first of its kind in Minnesota.

Throughout the 1980s and 1990s railroad employment fell. As new and improved technology was developed, jobs such as clerks and depot agents fell to computerization and new labor agreements. The number of crew persons fell from as many as five down to two: an engineer and conductor. Brakemen were eliminated because the caboose was no longer needed.

Cabooses housed crew members who would observe the cars ahead for defects, handle paperwork, operate track switches, monitor the brake system, observe if the train was moving or stopped as in-

tended by the engineer, and apply the brakes in an emergency. Now defect observation has been taken over by trackside detectors, the conductor does paperwork in the locomotive, and many (although not all) switches are thrown by remote control. The caboose's other functions are now performed by an end-of-train (EOT) device, a small metal box with a flashing light on the rear coupler of the last car. It monitors the brakes and has sensors that determine motion of the rear end. Radio transmissions from the EOT device tell the engineer if the rear end is stopped or moving forward or backward. A two-way telemetry system allows the EOT device to apply the train brakes on radio command from the train crew, which can be necessary in emergencies. A few cabooses remain on certain runs that perform a lot of switching, make extended backup moves, or use lots of passing sidings with manual switches.[28]

Twenty years after the upheaval of the Rock Island shutdown and Milwaukee embargo of 1980, Minnesota's railroads presented a completely different picture. There were fewer miles of track, but those that remained were well maintained and carried more traffic. The large railroads of 1980—Burlington Northern, Chicago & North Western, Milwaukee Road, and Soo Line had morphed into BNSF Railway, Canadian Pacific, and Union Pacific. Lines that once might have been abandoned were operated by short line and regional railroads. Railroads, once spurned by investors as a declining industry, had become an attractive investment—so much so, that in the twenty-first century one of the most successful investors in the world would stake $34 billion on the industry's success.

A kinder fate than liquidation awaited the Rock Island's competitor, Milwaukee Road. In bankruptcy since 1977, its trustees decided to embargo much of the system, retrenching from a 9,800-mile transcontinental to a Midwest-only railroad of approximately 4,700 miles (later reduced even further), an action unprecedented in American railroading. On embargo day, February 29, 1980, the last local from Jackson to Madison, South Dakota, rolls past the abandoned station at Hatfield. Photograph by Steve Glischinski.

In June 1982 the downsized Milwaukee Road and Canadian National's Duluth, Winnipeg & Pacific began run-through freight train service between Chicago and Winnipeg. The trains were established in anticipation of a possible acquisition of the Milwaukee Road by Canadian National subsidiary Grand Trunk Corporation. The Milwaukee Road moved the trains from Chicago to Duluth, where they were interchanged to the Duluth, Winnipeg & Pacific. On June 23, 1983, a northbound run-through train approaches the drawbridge over St. Louis Bay connecting Superior, Wisconsin, and Duluth. In the background the steamer *William A. McGonagle* is moored at a grain elevator in Superior. Photograph by Steve Glischinski.

The last passenger train to ever visit Ely heads out of town on September 19, 1981. The railroad came to Ely in 1888, and the Duluth, Missabe & Iron Range served iron ore mines in the area until the last one closed in 1967. The Missabe continued to serve the few non-ore industries in town with local freight trains, but declining business brought an end to that service, and the line was pulled up in 1982. This passenger special made a round-trip from Tower to Ely and back as the annual autumn rail excursion of the Minnesota Section of the American Institute of Mining, Metallurgical and Petroleum Engineers (AIME). Photograph by Steve Glischinski.

[OPPOSITE, ABOVE] The Minneapolis, Northfield & Southern ran its last trains in June 1982. It had earned its profits from industrial traffic in the western suburbs of Minneapolis and by serving as a bypass around the Twin Cities. But its connections at Northfield, the Milwaukee Road and Rock Island, had fallen on hard times, which reduced traffic levels. Soo Line was making an effort to purchase the former Rock Island line to Kansas City and bought the Minneapolis, Northfield & Southern to connect with it in Northfield. Chicago & North Western got the route instead, and the Minneapolis, Northfield & Southern became a branch for the Soo. Just before the end, Minneapolis, Northfield & Southern's *High Line* local job heads through the Hyland Lake Park Reserve in Bloomington on June 1, 1982.

[OPPOSITE, BELOW] Chicago & North Western train 164 from Oelwein, Iowa, is crossing the Cannon River at Randolph on May 4, 1980. Trains have been running on this line since 1885, but the end is near. Chicago & North Western is already leasing the parallel Rock Island route between Inver Grove Heights and Albert Lea and will soon buy it, which will render this former Chicago Great Western line redundant. The last train south of Randolph will run on November 6, 1981. Photograph by Steve Glischinski.

[RIGHT] In 1983, the Chicago & North Western outbid the Soo Line and purchased the Rock Island main line from the Twin Cities to Kansas City and several Iowa branches for $93 million. The company then began investing in upgrades, installing welded rail and new rock ballast to raise train speeds. In 1986, Chicago & North Western officers inspected their new line using the company's business car train. Looking like the *400* streamliners of old, the train passes the soon-to-be-demolished Rock Island passenger depot in Owatonna on October 15, 1986. Photograph by Steve Glischinski.

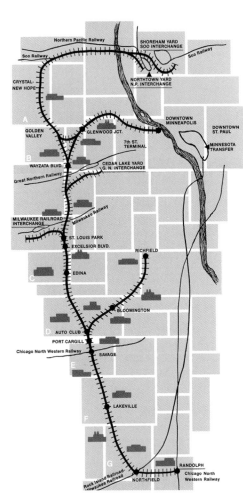

In the late 1960s the Minneapolis, Northfield & Southern issued a brochure to attract shippers that included this map illustrating the various points where it connected with larger railroads. Author's collection.

When this Chicago & North Western train crossed the trestle over Cherry Creek at Ottawa in March 1981, the railroad was on the cusp of major changes. It was a survivor, outlasting the Rock Island and avoiding bankruptcy like neighbor Milwaukee Road. In 1984, the North Western entered the coal-rich Powder River Basin in Wyoming. Coal revenues paid for new locomotives—the newest engine on this train was built in 1969—and allowed the company to rebuild the railroad. This wood trestle is one beneficiary, rebuilt with concrete and steel to handle heavy coal trains. Photograph by Steve Glischinski.

From 1975 to 1985, the State of Minnesota sponsored Amtrak service between Minneapolis and the Twin Ports, reviving a passenger route that ended in 1971. Dubbed the *Arrowhead,* it made its first run on April 16, 1975. In April 1978 the train was extended to Chicago and renamed *North Star*. Cutbacks in funding severed the Chicago service in 1981, but the St. Paul–Duluth train hung on until Easter Sunday 1985, when state funding ran out. In June 1984 a short *North Star* passes Duluth, Missabe & Iron Range's docks and several retired Great Lakes steamers. Photograph by Steve Glischinski.

The Illinois Central Railroad was a minor player in Minnesota railroading. It had two branch lines in the state: from Waterloo, Iowa, to Albert Lea; and from Fort Dodge, Iowa, to Sioux Falls, South Dakota, which nicked the far southwest corner of the state and passed through the tiny towns of Steen and Hills. In 1972 it was renamed Illinois Central Gulf following its merger with the Gulf, Mobile & Ohio. On April 4, 1980, there's still plenty of snow as Illinois Central Gulf train 572 departs Albert Lea for Waterloo. The train is running on the former Rock Island, which shut down four days before, and will reach home rails in seven miles at Glenville. Photograph by Steve Glischinski.

The Green Bay & Western, or Green Bay Route, had a minimal presence in Minnesota, serving only Winona. The railroad crossed Wisconsin from Winona to Wisconsin Rapids and Green Bay and then on to the Lake Michigan port of Kewaunee. It was a bridge line with much of its traffic originating and terminating off-line. To reach Winona, Green Bay & Western crossed the Mississippi River on a bridge jointly owned with the Burlington Route through a separate entity, the Winona Bridge Railway Company. Opened in July 1891, the bridge remained in service until 1985. It was damaged by a fire in December 1989 and then dismantled. On April 9, 1981, train 2 for Green Bay crosses the ninety-year-old structure. Photograph by Gene Hetherington.

[ABOVE] The ability of railroads to abandon lines became easier with deregulation, and Burlington Northern took full advantage of the opportunity, abandoning approximately 649 miles of line in Minnesota between 1980 and 1990. One of the largest was the 194-mile line from Brainerd to International Falls, abandoned in 1985. Its main function had been to move traffic to and from paper mills in International Falls. Burlington Northern gained trackage rights from Superior, Wisconsin, to International Falls on the Duluth, Winnipeg & Pacific to replace it. On March 10, 1985, a southbound is crossing the trestle over Walker Bay of Leech Lake at Ah-Gwah-Ching. Photograph by Steve Glischinski.

[OPPOSITE, ABOVE] On April 19, 1985, Soo Line ran its last through train from Bemidji to Superior, Wisconsin. It was abandoning the lightly trafficked route in favor of trackage rights over a parallel Burlington Northern line. A string of forty-foot boxcars is rolling across the Mississippi River at Palisade as the last train heads east. Like the rails they are running on, forty-foot boxcars will soon be a thing of the past, replaced by fifty- and sixty-foot, higher-capacity cars. Photograph by Steve Glischinski.

[OPPOSITE, BELOW] There were few depots remaining in regular service in the 1980s and 1990s. As railroads adopted newer technology to deliver orders to trains, depot operators were phased out, as were the buildings themselves. If a building happened to be built with brick, it usually survived, but that wasn't the case for the depot at Elbow Lake. Opened in 1916, it was dismantled in January 1987. Westbound freight 91 is passing the building on a beautiful afternoon in July 1986. An identical Soo depot was preserved as a museum at Osceola, Wisconsin. Photograph by Tom Carlson.

[LEFT, ABOVE] Fortunately many towns worked to preserve their depots as railroads retired them. Several railroads were generous in donating depots to communities or offering them at a reduced price. An example is the former Northern Pacific depot in Aitkin. Built in 1916, it was donated to the Aitkin County Historical Society by Burlington Northern in 1976. An eastbound Burlington Northern freight is passing the building on September 14, 1985. Photograph by Steve Glischinski.

[LEFT, BELOW] The Northern Pacific depot in Little Falls has a notable pedigree: it was designed by famed architect Cass Gilbert, who also designed the Minnesota State Capitol, the U.S. Supreme Court Building in Washington, D.C., and the Woolworth Building in New York. Work on the depot began in 1899 and was completed on January 30, 1900. The last passenger train stopped there in 1971. Placed on the National Register of Historic Places in 1985, it was donated to the Cass Gilbert Depot Society by Burlington Northern in 1988. On February 26, 1978, an eastbound piggyback train passes the depot. Photograph by Steve Glischinski.

[OPPOSITE] In the late 1980s and early 1990s the iconic railroad caboose fell to changes in technology and new labor agreements that reduced the number of personnel operating trains. Cabooses were replaced by an end-of-train device, a small metal box with a flashing light on the rear coupler of the last car. The device monitors systems and communicates telemetry to the locomotive. While these devices are efficient, they have none of the romance of the caboose—it's no fun waving at a metal box. In September 1985 two crewmen look from a Burlington Northern caboose passing through Brainerd. Photograph by Steve Glischinski.

[ABOVE] On January 4, 1985, a Milwaukee Road switch engine pauses between chores beside the office at South Minneapolis Yard, just south of downtown. A busy location in the steam era, with its own shop and roundhouse, the yard was downgraded in the 1990s and eventually removed. No trace of it is visible today. Metro Transit's Hiawatha Light Rail Line uses much of the right-of-way through the old yard area. Photograph by Steve Glischinski; lighting by Robert M. Ball.

[OPPOSITE, BELOW] The Soo Line's route from Thief River Falls to Kenmare, North Dakota, was known as the Wheat Line. In a 1905 ad the railroad bragged that it was "295 Miles of the Richest Wheat Raising Country in the U.S." The Soo and successor Canadian Pacific operated the Wheat Line until 1997, when it was leased to the Northern Plains Railroad. On August 20, 1986, eight months after the Milwaukee Road was fully integrated into the Soo, a train of empty grain hoppers is crossing the Red River of the North heading into North Dakota at Oslo with a Milwaukee Road diesel up front. Photograph by George A. Forero Jr.

[ABOVE, LEFT] The tower in Newport was different from others in the state. It housed train dispatchers who controlled the jointly operated route between Division Street in St. Paul and St. Croix Tower in Hastings used by the Milwaukee Road and Burlington Route (Burlington Northern after 1970). Rock Island also used this line from Newport to St. Paul, crossing the Mississippi River from Inver Grove Heights on a swing bridge. The tower was built in 1906 by the Milwaukee Road. On September 19, 1984, the last day the tower was open, a dispatcher jots down an order as he contemplates a change in employment. Photograph by Steve Glischinski.

[ABOVE, RIGHT] That evening motorists are oblivious to the end of seventy-eight years of railroad tradition as they streak by the tower on adjacent Highway 61. The city of Newport, Newport businessmen, and the Greater East Area Model Railroad Club were instrumental in saving the structure, and it was moved on December 11, 1984, to a site on the west side of the tracks only a few blocks from where it once stood. Photograph by Steve Glischinski.

Minnesota steam fans in the 1980s had to be content with a handful of smaller locomotives that were serviceable. One was former Soo Line 0-6-0 No. 353, built in 1920. One of two engines sold by Soo to Kopper's Coke in St. Paul, it remained in service into the early 1960s, when it was acquired by the Minnesota Transportation Museum. In 1972 it was sold and restored to service by the Western Minnesota Steam Threshers. Each Labor Day Weekend, No. 353 operates at the Steam Threshers Reunion at Rollag on a short loop of track pulling passenger-carrying boxcars. It is running at the Reunion on September 4, 1989. Photograph by Steve Glischinski.

In 1981, Northern Pacific 4-6-0 No. 328, which once pulled trains on the Taylors Falls Branch, was returned to service by the Minnesota Transportation Museum after a five-year effort. Ordered in 1905 by the Chicago Southern Railroad, it was completed in 1907 by American Locomotive Company's Rogers Works and delivered to the Northern Pacific. It was retired in 1950 and displayed in a Stillwater park. The engine was partially submerged in the flooding waters of the St. Croix River in 1965. No. 328 poses with a Northern Pacific caboose at New Brighton on July 5, 1981, during its first weekend of excursion service. It operated until 1999. Photograph by Steve Glischinski.

[LEFT, ABOVE] Beginning in 1982, the Chicago & North Western began operating 4-6-0 No. 1385 on goodwill trips around its system. The brainchild of North Western manager Chris Burger, the locomotive was borrowed from its owner, the Mid-Continent Railway Museum of North Freedom, Wisconsin. The engine visited Minnesota on at least two occasions in the 1980s. No. 1385, which dates to 1907, rides the turntable at Minneapolis Junction on May 19, 1986. The roundhouse originally belonged to Great Northern and successor Burlington Northern. It was leased to the Chicago & North Western in the 1980s to replace its Cedar Lake Shops, which were demolished. Photograph by Steve Glischinski.

[LEFT, BELOW] The 1980s and 1990s saw the creation of regional railroads on lines sold by larger railroads. One of the more successful was Wisconsin Central Ltd., created in October 1987. It took over Soo Line's original routes in Wisconsin and Upper Michigan, plus two former Milwaukee Road lines. Under the leadership of former Chicago & North Western executive Ed Burkhardt, Wisconsin Central prospered. It owned little track in Minnesota, reaching the Twin Cities on trackage rights over the Soo. It was known for its colorful locomotive fleet, such as these rare (only eighty-six were built) EMD F45s meeting on Canadian Pacific track at Cardigan Junction in Shoreview on February 5, 1996. Photograph by Steve Glischinski.

[OPPOSITE, ABOVE] A 1980s phenomenon was the dinner train, which played on the nostalgia of eating in the diner while watching America pass by your window. The first successful dinner train began in 1985 when the Cedar Valley Railroad began operating the *Star Clipper* out of Osage, Iowa. It ran on a rotating schedule, starting its run out of different towns each week. Heading to Glenville to pick up diners, the *Star Clipper* is about to cross the Milwaukee Road at Lyle on July 5, 1985. It's flying U.S. flags to celebrate the Independence Day weekend. Photograph by Steve Glischinski.

[OPPOSITE, BELOW] The first dinner train came to Minnesota in 1986. Dakota Rail took over operation of the Burlington Northern line between Wayzata and Hutchinson on December 5, 1985. In September 1986, the railroad began operating the *Minnetonka Zephyr* out of Spring Park. The following year the *Zephyr* moved to Stillwater after the railroad and the train's owner could not agree on operating costs. Dakota Rail began its own operation, dubbed the *Hiawatha Dinner Train*, originating at either Spring Park or Hutchinson. The railroad's financial troubles ended service in July 1989. The train is heading west near Mound on December 27, 1987. Photograph by Steve Glischinski.

![DM&E Enroute masthead]

DM&E Enroute

June 1989

News for employees of DAKOTA, MINNESOTA & EASTERN RAILROAD CORP.

Trackwork progress

New ties, surfacing for South Dakota main line

Dakota, Minnesota & Eastern's main line is looking better each day as railroad and contractor crews rehabilitate the 362 miles of track across South Dakota by installing new ties, ballast, and surfacing.

Mike Arter, vice president and chief engineer, says, "A DM&E crew has put in ties on eight miles of track between Rapid City and Box Elder. United Railroad Services has installed ties between Box Elder and Wasta." New ballast is being applied at the rate of eight cars per mile. DM&E crews are surfacing the track, following the tie gang as it works eastward from Rapid City. Ballast has also been dumped at Highmore siding which, Arter says, was completed June 12.

Meanwhile, American Railroad Builders began installing ties near the state

line at Verdi, Minn. and is now working west through Elkton, S.D. to Brookings and Huron. They began at Lake Benton, Minn. in early April to complete a segment of the Minnesota 803 project.

DM&E's newly surfaced main line at Milepost 266 near Verdi, Minn. and the last curve for more than 28 miles until Sioux Valley Jct., S.D.

The trackwork in South Dakota is a two-year, $9 million program, largely financed by a $7.8 million Federal Railroad Administration loan, enabling the railroad to raise maximum train speeds to at least 25 miles per hour over most of the line.

In other work, DM&E forces have renewed the 4th Street crossing at Wall, S.D. Flashing crossing protection signals will be installed later this summer, Arter says. DM&E forces have begun work on state-financed grade crossing projects between Huron and Rapid City.

Grain shipments to Winona help to ease traffic declines

Carloadings down 24% from 1988

Carloadings on DM&E, totaling 3,319 in May, continue to lag from ... "We're running about 4,100 cars, or 2... of 1988," says Lynn An... the railr... cars less...

Last ... wheat ... gram h... concer... DM&E... from ... Gra...

source of traffic. The Garnac Grain Co. elevator, which is expanding its facility to accommodate up to 50 cars, resumed operations in early April. A second operator, Modern Transport Terminal, opened its new 25-car facil... the first week of May.

... shipments to barge facilities at ... of the corn via

[LEFT] Many of the new regional railroads of the 1980s and 1990s, unlike the larger railroads, tried to establish good relationships with their employees. The Dakota, Minnesota & Eastern used the *Enroute* newsletter to keep its employees informed. Author's collection.

[BELOW] Among the new railroads of the 1980s was the Dakota, Minnesota & Eastern. In 1986, it took over Chicago & North Western's route across southern Minnesota, part of a line that reached six hundred miles from Winona to Rapid City, South Dakota. Unfortunately it inherited poorly maintained track from the North Western, and its early years were plagued by costly derailments and large expenditures to get track back in shape. By the time Dakota, Minnesota & Eastern was purchased by Canadian Pacific in October 2008, the railroad was profitable and much of its track had seen new ties and rail. On January 6, 1991, an eastbound Dakota, Minnesota & Eastern train is passing the preserved Chicago & North Western passenger depot at Sleepy Eye. Photograph by Steve Glischinski.

When EMD celebrated its fiftieth anniversary in 1990, it repainted FT 103, the famous diesel that had made a barnstorming tour in 1939 and 1940 that convinced many railroads to buy diesels. After a gathering at La Grange, Illinois, No. 103 was made available to museums for temporary display, and in the summer of 1990 it traveled to Duluth's Lake Superior Railroad Museum. A special photo session was held with 103 and Great Northern 400, the first production SD45 from 1966. The two engines pose outside the museum on July 3, 1990, as a lake boat passes under the famous Aerial Lift Bridge. Photograph by Steve Glischinski.

[ABOVE] The Otter Tail Valley Railroad is a short line spinoff that took over Burlington Northern's line from Moorhead to St. Cloud in October 1986. Ninety percent of the railroad's business was between Moorhead and Fergus Falls, and in 1991 Otter Tail Valley Railroad abandoned the ninety-six miles of railroad east of Fergus Falls. Once a secondary line of the Great Northern and successor Burlington Northern, it was laid with heavy rail, which Burlington Northern was anxious to reclaim. A special train picks up rail near West Union on July 8, 1992—the last train to ever visit the town. Photograph by Steve Glischinski.

[OPPOSITE] Otter Tail Valley's largest customer is the Otter Tail Power Company Hoot Lake Power Plant at Fergus Falls, which receives unit trains of coal. On May 11, 1994, the short line is debuting a new black and white paint scheme on locomotive 192 pulling empty cars out of the plant. Photograph by Steve Glischinski.

[LEFT] Otter Tail Valley was owned by Anacostia & Pacific Company from 1986 to 1996, when short line railroad conglomerate RailAmerica purchased the company and issued this marketing brochure. Author's collection.

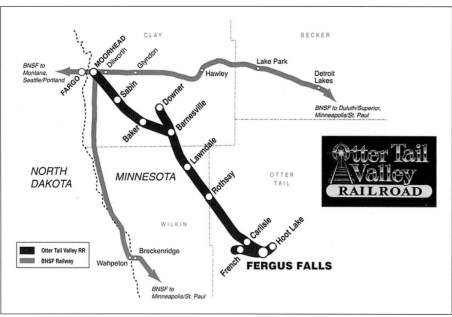

[OPPOSITE, ABOVE] The last of Minnesota's logging railroads operating under its original name is the Minnesota, Dakota & Western Railway. It operates six miles of track between International Falls, Ranier, and Fort Frances, Ontario, via the International Bridge, which it shares with automobiles. Dating to 1910, it was incorporated in 1902 as the International Bridge and Terminal Company. Boise Inc. owns Minnesota, Dakota & Western, which serves paper mills in both International Falls and Fort Frances. Tucked away in its engine house in International Falls are three of the line's Alco switch engines, protected from the elements on the night of January 27, 1995. Photograph by Steve Glischinski.

[OPPOSITE, BELOW] In the summer of 1989, Soo Line adopted a new color scheme for its diesel fleet. Called "candy apple red," the solid color was intended to provide a cleaner appearance. It also used reflectorized lettering intended to increase visibility. At the suggestion of locomotive engineer Gene Hetherington, reflective stripes were added to the nose. The Shoreham paint shop crew of Ron Kulke and Joe Sykes pose in Minneapolis with SD40-2 No. 772, the second locomotive to be painted red and the first to receive the nose stripes. In the 1990s Soo Line successor Canadian Pacific chose to centralize locomotive maintenance at St. Paul, closing the Shoreham shops. Collection of Stuart J. Nelson.

[ABOVE] Canadian Pacific Railway had long held 56 percent of Soo Line's stock but allowed the company to operate independently. In the late 1980s it decided to sell the Soo, but then it reversed course and instead bought full control of the company in 1990. It gradually extinguished the Soo Line brand, bringing Canadian Pacific equipment, locomotives, and management to the Soo. Soo Line still exists on paper, and many of its locomotives were slow to be repainted, but scenes such as this Soo train crossing the Pomme de Terre River at Barrett in 1990 are impossible to repeat. Photograph by Tom Carlson.

[LEFT, ABOVE] Another railroad absorbed by its larger Canadian parent was Duluth, Winnipeg & Pacific. The 167-mile railroad reached from Fort Frances, Ontario, to Duluth, and had been owned by Canadian National since 1917. It served as Canadian National's conduit into the northern United States, exchanging traffic with other railroads in Duluth and, after a relocation in 1984, Superior, Wisconsin. In 1992, Canadian National began marketing its U.S. subsidiaries as part of its system and integrated operations in 1996, ending Duluth, Winnipeg & Pacific's independence. Photographed from a mine waste hill, Duluth, Winnipeg & Pacific train 313 is about to cross the Duluth, Missabe & Iron Range just south of Virginia on September 21, 1991. Photograph by Steve Glischinski.

[LEFT, BELOW] Crossing into Canada from the United States, a special excursion train celebrating the U.S. Bicentennial crosses the Duluth, Winnipeg & Pacific bridge over the Rainy River at Ranier on August 7, 1976. While trains used to endure lengthy inspections at the border, changes in customs regulations and the installation of a large X-ray machine eliminated long waits. Photograph by Steve Glischinski.

[OPPOSITE, ABOVE] The Minnesota Commercial Railway, based in St. Paul, began operations on the former Minnesota Transfer Railway on February 1, 1987. Incorporated in 1883, the Transfer was owned by the railroads serving the Twin Cities. It had over 150 miles of yard and industrial track and handled between 2,500 and 3,500 cars daily in the 1950s. Most of its business was interchange between railroads, but that declined as more were merged out of existence. The three surviving owners decided to spin off the Minnesota Transfer to the Minnesota Commercial. Since then, it has expanded beyond the area once served by the Transfer. It took over Burlington Northern's route to Hugo in 1990. The *Hugo Job* passes the White Bear Lake depot on December 21, 1994. Photograph by Steve Glischinski.

[OPPOSITE, BELOW] In 1998, Minnesota Commercial took over switching operations from Burlington Northern & Santa Fe Railway at the Pillsbury A Mill elevator in Minneapolis. This included some of the oldest surviving track in the state, dating to 1862 when the St. Paul & Pacific operated the first train in Minnesota. Two freshly painted General Electric locomotives are switching at the mill in December 1999. The mill ceased operation in 2003. Photograph by Steve Glischinski.

1991 saw the birth of a new railroad, the Twin Cities & Western, based in Glencoe. Twin Cities & Western's line once was part of Milwaukee Road's route from the Twin Cities to Seattle/Tacoma and was purchased from Canadian Pacific's Soo Line subsidiary. Operations began in July 1991 when it acquired 147 miles of track between Hopkins and Appleton. The railroad also operates into St. Paul and to Sisseton, South Dakota, on other railroads. Ribbon-cutting ceremonies marking the startup of operations were held in Glencoe on August 4, 1991, the same day a train headed past Duck Lake in Eden Prairie for St. Paul. Photograph by Steve Glischinski.

The Rush City–based St. Croix Valley Railroad was created in September 1997 when Burlington Northern and Santa Fe sold two lines: thirty-six miles between Hinckley and North Branch, and eleven miles between Brook Park and Mora. The buyer was RailAmerica, which owns a number of short line and regional railroads in North America. In 2001, St. Croix Valley was sold to KBN Incorporated and Independent Locomotive Service, which also co-owns Minnesota Northern. In RailAmerica days, a train moves off the Mora Line at Brook Park and onto Burlington Northern and Santa Fe for the short run to Hinckley on May 19, 1999. The Mora Line was abandoned in 2003. Photograph by Steve Glischinski.

[OPPOSITE, ABOVE] On the Mesabi Iron Range several taconite plants used railroads to move raw ore from mines to crushing facilities, where it was broken up for processing into taconite pellets. US Steel's Minntac Plant at Mountain Iron is the biggest producer in Minnesota and had one of the largest rail operations. Contained within the huge complex was a mostly double-track, signal-equipped railroad that operated twenty-four hours a day. On July 1, 1997, a train is loading at Minntac's East Pit while another train is seen above, making its way out of the pit. Photograph by Steve Glischinski.

[OPPOSITE, BELOW] Minntac had a large shop to maintain and overhaul its fleet of diesel switchers and cars. A worker is inspecting Minntac 967 at the shop in July 1997. As pits grew deeper and more tracks had to be laid, the cost of rail transportation and the time it took for trains to reach the crusher increased. In 1999 Minntac abandoned rail operations in favor of trucks. The last train operated on November 29, 1999. The rails were torn up, the locomotives were sold, and the shop was converted to truck maintenance. Photograph by Steve Glischinski.

[ABOVE] In the 1990s Wisconsin Central landed a contract to move taconite pellets from the Minntac Plant to Geneva Steel in Vineyard, Utah, in partnership with Duluth, Missabe & Iron Range and Southern Pacific. The moves brought Southern Pacific locomotives to Minnesota as the trains ran through from Chicago with the western railroad's locomotives. An empty Wisconsin Central ore train with Southern Pacific locomotives arrives at Duluth, Missabe & Iron Range's Steelton Yard in the Gary/New Duluth neighborhood of Duluth on September 29, 1994. Photograph by Steve Glischinski.

[ABOVE] The 1980s brought tough times to Reserve Mining Company. In June 1986, Reserve shut down following the bankruptcy of LTV Steel, one of its owners, which concentrated its production at neighboring Erie Mining, also owned by LTV Steel. After sitting dormant for four years, it reopened under the ownership of Cyprus Minerals and was renamed Cyprus Northshore Mining. Trains began running again on the forty-seven-mile railroad on January 5, 1990. Cyprus Northshore Mining was sold to Cleveland Cliffs (now Cliffs Natural Resources) in 1994, and the name was changed to Cliffs Northshore Mining. Four former Reserve Mining diesels lug an empty Cyprus train out of the Lake Superior Basin on June 12, 1991. Photograph by Steve Glischinski.

[OPPOSITE, ABOVE] A railroad that came back from the dead was the route between Duluth and Two Harbors. Unused since 1984, it was purchased by St. Louis and Lake County Regional Rail Authority from the Duluth, Missabe & Iron Range in 1988. Now the North Shore Scenic Railroad, it operates tourist trains using volunteers and equipment from Duluth's Lake Superior Railroad Museum. When operations began in 1990, Duluth–Two Harbors runs were made with a rail diesel car—the same equipment the Missabe Road had been using over the line when passenger service ended in 1961. The rail diesel car prepares to depart Two Harbors on August 5, 1990. Photograph by Steve Glischinski.

[OPPOSITE, BELOW] Burlington Northern was one of the largest grain-hauling railroads in the United States. At the Twin Ports of Duluth and Superior the grain is loaded into lake boats and ocean-going vessels. Seen from a fire tower at Nickerson, a Burlington Northern grain train heads south from the Twin Ports on July 10, 1994. New grain cars trail the locomotives. Photograph by Steve Glischinski.

[ABOVE] The heaviest trains on Minnesota railroads are not coal but taconite trains operated by Burlington Northern and successor BNSF Railway. These trains can run up to 180 cars and weigh over 24,000 tons— some of the heaviest trains in North America. On September 19, 1994, the leaves are starting to change color as one of the massive trains crosses the Husan Bridge near Wrenshall, heading to the Hibbing Taconite Plant for another load of taconite. Photograph by Steve Glischinski.

[OPPOSITE] The largest railroad in Minnesota is BNSF Railway, the result of the September 22, 1995, merger of Burlington Northern Inc. with the Santa Fe Pacific Corporation. Their railroad subsidiaries, Burlington Northern Railroad and Atchison, Topeka & Santa Fe Railway, merged on December 31, 1996. Initially named Burlington Northern and Santa Fe Railway, the name was simplified to BNSF Railway in January 2005. BNSF revived the orange colors that Great Northern dropped in 1967, although BNSF used several variations and striping patterns over the years. Two just-delivered BNSF diesels cross the Kettle River in Sandstone on September 9, 1996. Photograph by Steve Glischinski.

[LEFT, ABOVE] Probably the most famous paint scheme worn by a diesel locomotive was the red and silver Santa Fe Warbonnet. Reminiscent of a Native American ceremonial headdress, it dates to 1937, when Santa Fe used the colors on new diesels for its Chicago–Los Angeles *Super Chief* passenger train. Discontinued in 1971, Santa Fe president Mike Haverty revived the Warbonnet colors in 1989. After the BNSF merger, the new railroad initially retained the scheme, but with standardization in vogue, it quietly dropped them in favor of orange and green. Some of the last Warbonnet diesels were delivered in 1997, such as these two locomotives passing through St. Paul on October 22 on their first trip. Photograph by Steve Glischinski.

[LEFT, BELOW] Chicago & North Western lost its independence in 1995, when Union Pacific purchased it. The two had long enjoyed a close relationship. Union Pacific sent trains from Omaha to Chicago over the North Western and partnered with Chicago & North Western to finance an expansion into Wyoming coal country in 1984. A decade later the North Western was a profitable railroad ripe for merger. It went out on a high note, purchasing 165 new GE locomotives in 1994 and 1995 that wore its yellow colors dating to the *Twin Cities 400* of 1939. Two of the new machines head south at Brook Park, using rights over Burlington Northern on May 31, 1994. Photograph by Steve Glischinski.

[OPPOSITE, RIGHT] One of the best examples of the ever-changing nature of railroading can be found along the former Milwaukee Road in southern Minnesota. These routes have changed ownership multiple times since 1985. In 1985, Soo Line purchased the Milwaukee Road. Canadian Pacific acquired the Soo in 1990. In 1997, Canadian Pacific sold several of its ex–Milwaukee Road lines in southern Minnesota and Iowa and its Chicago–Kansas City route to the new I&M Rail Link. The I&M Rail Link was not profitable, and in July 2002 it was sold to another new railroad, Iowa, Chicago & Eastern. Canadian Pacific then purchased Iowa, Chicago & Eastern in 2008, returning the lines to the Canadian Pacific fold. During the short-lived I&M Rail Link era, intermodal train 99 meets a barge along the Mississippi River at Brownsville on October 14, 1999. Photograph by Steve Glischinski.

[ABOVE] The railroad preservation movement gained steam through the 1980s and 1990s. Enthusiastic volunteers restored steam locomotives that had been rusting away on display for decades. Their work made possible this scene at Marine on St. Croix on August 2, 1998. Three steam locomotives—Northern Pacific 328 and Soo Line 2719 and 1003, all once display engines—are roaring past photographers with an excursion sponsored by the Minnesota Transportation Museum. It was the first time a steam locomotive tripleheader had run in the state since the 1950s. Photograph by Steve Glischinski.

Minnesota railroads in the twenty-first century are profitable companies that continually invest in their physical property and rolling stock to handle increasing levels of traffic. Confidence in railroading's future was demonstrated in a public way when billionaire investor Warren Buffett purchased BNSF Railway on February 12, 2010. The fresh face of railroading is on display as three spanking new BNSF locomotives roll west near Lake Park on March 28, 2010. The multimillion-dollar diesels are making their first trip from builder General Electric's Erie, Pennsylvania, plant pulling an ethanol train, new business that didn't exist just a few years before. Photograph by Steve Glischinski.

4

Railroading in the Twenty-First Century

RAILROADS IN THE TWENTY-FIRST CENTURY are profitable, growing enterprises that handled 42 percent of all intercity commercial freight in 2007,[1] a far cry from the 1960s and 1970s when the industry struggled to survive. Railroads have plowed money back into their physical plant—no longer are railroads forced to defer maintenance. According to Union Pacific, the largest publicly held U.S. railroad, it spent over $28 billion on infrastructure between 2000 and 2010 and spent a record $3.3 billion in 2011 on improvements. Overall, in 2011 U.S. railroads spent close to $12 billion on infrastructure and equipment.[2]

One of the biggest growth areas has been in intermodal container traffic. Intermodal is defined as moving freight using multiple modes of transport (such as rail, truck, or ship) without handling the freight itself when changing between the modes. The Association of American Railroads reported that the intermodal revenue at the five top U.S. railroads—BNSF Railway, CSX Transportation, Kansas City Southern, Norfolk Southern, and Union Pacific—rose to $11.3 billion in 2010 from $6.9 billion in 2000.[3]

Most intermodal business moves from East or West Coast ports cross-country or to intermodal hub centers, such as those on BNSF in St. Paul and Canadian Pacific in Minneapolis. Domestic intermodal business is expected to increase because of the inherent efficiency of rail transportation: it can be cheaper than long-distance trucking, and it is more fuel-efficient.[4] While most trains and trucks run on diesel fuel, trains use a quarter the amount of fuel a truck does to haul a comparable amount of cargo. This is because the steel wheels of railroad cars running on steel tracks create less resistance than rubber tires on concrete roads and because freight locomotives run on diesel-electric power, which is relatively more efficient than a straight diesel engine. According to the Association of American Railroads, in 2010, per gallon of fuel, U.S. railroads moved a ton of freight an average of 484 miles.

Unlike in the 1950s and 1960s, in the twenty-first century truck transport faces a lack of highway capacity, higher fuel prices, highway congestion, and tighter government regulations. By contrast, railroads have the ability to add their own capacity along their private rights-of-way, are more fuel-efficient, and were freed of much regulation in the 1980s. Trucks will remain the dominant carrier of short-haul freight, but railroads are taking over the longer hauls. Since a train can carry the freight of 280 or more trucks, it is more economical and fuel-efficient to ship by rail on longer hauls.[5]

Railroads have become so successful that they have been become the target of investors. Renowned investor Warren Buffett, through his investment company Berkshire Hathaway Inc., purchased BNSF Railway in February 2010 for $44 billion, the largest purchase in Berkshire history.[6] In 2011, Microsoft Corporation cofounder Bill Gates was the largest shareholder in Canadian National Railway, owning shares worth $3.2 billion.[7]

As larger railroads became more successful, they looked at ways to expand. Among their targets were regional railroads that sprang up in the 1980s and 1990s following deregulation. They began buying and integrating the regional lines into their systems, including several that served Minnesota. Canadian National Railway was a leader in this area, acquiring the Wisconsin Central in October 2001 and the Duluth, Missabe & Iron Range in May 2004. Canadian Pacific purchased the Dakota, Minnesota & Eastern and Iowa, Chicago & Eastern in October 2008 and began a slow assimilation of the two railroads into its system.

Short line railroads continue to be a growth business in the twenty-first century. In 2001, the Minnesota Southern Railway began operations. It runs forty-one miles of former Chicago & North Western track from a connection with Union Pacific near Worthington to a connection with BNSF at Manley. The railroad is owned by the Buffalo Ridge Rail Authority and leased to Minnesota Southern.

Progressive Rail, which began operations in Lakeville in 1996, expanded in 2004, taking over the former Minneapolis, Northfield & Southern main line from Lakeville to Northfield, the ex–Milwaukee Road line from Rosemount to Eagan, and two Union Pacific lines to Cannon Falls and Faribault. Progressive, in a salute to its heritage, paints its locomotives in the colors of the old Minneapolis, Northfield & Southern Railway, which was purchased by the Soo Line in 1982.

In 2005, the Northern Lines Railway was formed to operate twenty-three miles of former BNSF lines in the St. Cloud area. Anacostia & Pacific Company Inc., a transportation and development firm that has developed eight new railroads since it was formed in 1985, owns the railroad. Northern Lines operates out of the former Great Northern–Burlington Northern yard in St. Cloud and operates branch lines to St. Joseph and Cold Spring.

In 2012 there are nineteen railroads with track in Minnesota:

BNSF Railway (1,598 miles)
Canadian Pacific Railway (750 miles)
Canadian National Railway (436 miles)
Cloquet Terminal Railroad (4 miles)
Dakota, Minnesota & Eastern/Iowa, Chicago & Eastern (472 miles)

Minnesota Commercial Railway (35 miles)

Minnesota, Dakota & Western Railway (4 miles)

Minnesota Northern Railroad (156 miles)

Minnesota Prairie Line (94 miles)

Minnesota Southern Railroad (42 miles)

North Shore Scenic Railroad (25 miles)

Northern Lines Railway (23 miles)

Northern Plains Railroad (45 miles)

Otter Tail Valley Railroad (71 miles)

Progressive Rail Inc. (80 miles)

Red River Valley & Western Railroad (2 miles)

St. Croix Valley Railroad (36 miles)

Twin Cities & Western Railroad (146 miles)

Union Pacific Railroad (462 miles)[8]

In the first decade of the twenty-first century, a modest resurgence of passenger train transport began as travel on Amtrak grew and more cities turned to commuter and light rail as alternatives to automobiles. In Minnesota, 2004 saw the opening of the twelve-mile Hiawatha Light Rail Line between downtown Minneapolis, Minneapolis–St. Paul International Airport, and the Mall of America. A second Twin Cities light-rail line, which will link downtown Minneapolis and downtown St. Paul, began construction in 2010 with a planned opening in 2014.

Commuter trains returned to Minnesota for the first time since the early years of the twentieth century in 2009. On November 16, 2009, Northstar commuter rail service began between Minneapolis and Big Lake, operating over forty miles of BNSF Railway track. It began with five locomotives built by Motive Power Industries of Boise, Idaho, and seventeen double-deck cars constructed by Canada's Bombardier.

State and federal governments, the regional rail authorities for Anoka, Hennepin, and Sherburne counties, the Metropolitan Council, and the Minnesota Twins shared the $320 million cost of building the line.[9]

Northstar started with stops at six stations: Big Lake, Elk River, Anoka, Coon Rapids–Riverdale, Fridley, and downtown Minneapolis. The Minneapolis station is truly multimodal: an escalator ride takes passengers up to Fifth Street, where they can connect with Hiawatha Line trains.

When the commuter service was proposed in the 1990s, the line was expected to go from Minneapolis to St. Cloud, but changes in the transit funding formula from the federal government forced it to be cut back to Big Lake, with an extensive connecting bus service operating between St. Cloud and Big Lake.

On April 30, 1971, the St. Paul Union Depot saw its last passenger trains. Amtrak chose to use the Minneapolis Great Northern Station as its sole Twin Cities stop. That station was torn down in 1978 and replaced with a new depot in St. Paul's Midway area, but in 2012 the St. Paul Union Depot will replace that station.

The depot was designed by Charles Sumner Frost and constructed between 1917 and 1924. During its heyday it was served by nine railroads: Burlington, Chicago & North Western (Omaha Road), Chicago Great Western, Great Northern, Milwaukee Road, Minneapolis & St. Louis (which pulled out during the Great Depression), Northern Pacific, Rock Island, and Soo Line.

Unlike many big city railroad terminals that were recycled for other uses, the Union Depot remained relatively unchanged over the decades since the last trains departed. The head house of the structure was reworked with offices, restaurants, and condominium lofts. The U.S. Postal Service purchased the rear concourse over the tracks and train sheds. The sheds were torn down and the track area paved over. The concourse was left largely untouched, with most of its doors bricked up; it was used for storage.

Between 2005 and 2009 the Ramsey County Regional Rail Authority purchased the head house and concourse area from private companies and the Postal Service, gaining control of the entire structure. In January 2011 a $243-million renovation of the depot began in order to restore the facility to its original purpose as a transportation hub. The thirty-three-acre site will serve as a station for Amtrak, Jefferson bus lines, Metro Transit city bus routes, and the Central Corridor Light Rail Line from Minneapolis. The depot may also serve as a terminal for future commuter rail service and high-speed rail service to Chicago.

The Union Depot will be a rare revival of what many consider to be the golden age of railroading, but it's possible that age is yet to come. According to the Federal Highway Administration, U.S. freight shipments will rise from an estimated 16.9 billion tons in 2010 to 27.1 billion tons in 2040—a 61 percent increase. A good percentage of this increase will fall to the railroads to move, which will require huge capital investments. From 1980 to 2010, freight railroads invested some $480 billion on locomotives, freight cars, tracks, bridges, tunnels, and other infrastructure, and billions more will be needed in the future to keep up with demand.[10] Unlike deregulation in the late twentieth century, which helped to keep a struggling industry alive, in the twenty-first century the federal government may need to lend assistance to help a growing rail industry expand its infrastructure.

Minnesota railroads in the twenty-first century are thriving. As of 2009, there were twenty railroads in the state operating 4,528 miles of track. That places Minnesota eighth in total railroad miles by state. To carry the amount of freight Minnesota railroads moved in 2009 would have required 11.3 million trucks to move the same amount of traffic.

MINNESOTA RAILROADS AT A GLANCE	U.S. RANK
Rail Tons Originated: 67,383,000	6
Rail Tons Terminated: 60,186,000	14
Carloads Originated: 893,300	7
Carloads terminated: 800,100	11
Tons Carried (millions): 203.15	13
Carloads Carried: 2,994,400	18
Employment: 4,222	14[11]

In the future, railroads that serve Minnesota may become even larger. In 2011 there were seven Class 1 railroad systems that earned 2009 revenues of over $379 million: BNSF Railway, CSX Transportation, Canadian National, Canadian Pacific, Kansas City Southern, Norfolk Southern, and Union Pacific. For years, railroad observers have speculated that there will be a final round of mergers that will reduce the seven down to two transcontinental systems serving all of North America.

Even if there are someday only two mega railroads, they will remain vital to transportation. Railroads, which helped build Minnesota since the first line was built between St. Paul and St. Anthony in 1862, may once again take center stage in keeping Minnesota's economy growing in the twenty-first century.

Locomotive engineers have an array of computer screens and use desktop controls to operate their diesels. It's a far cry from the days of steam power, when engineers contended with the dirt from coal-fired engines and had to stick their heads out of windswept cabs. This is the cab of a General Electric 4,400-horsepower ES44DC locomotive. Photograph by Steve Glischinski.

Two types of energy delivery are on display near Holland on the evening of July 20, 1010. An empty BNSF coal train winds through the hills en route to Wyoming's Powder River Basin for another load of coal to be burned in power plants. Also generating power are the wind turbines in the background, placed along the hills of the Buffalo Ridge. The Ridge is a sixty-mile expanse of hills in the southwestern part of the state that stands 1,995 feet above sea level. Because of its altitude and high average wind speed, Buffalo Ridge has been transformed into a prime location for wind turbines. Photograph by John Leopard.

When railroads were first constructed, they tended to take the route of least resistance. This meant they often followed rivers and streams, since they allowed the railroad to use the natural topography of the waterway to cut across the land. The disadvantage was that when the waters overflowed their banks, the railroad was flooded. Even today, de- spite line relocations and embankments built up to elevate the right-of-way, railroads still must contend with floods, particularly in the spring. A BNSF Railway intermodal train is tiptoeing through the floodwaters of the Mississippi River at Hastings on April 27, 2001. Photograph by Steve Glischinski.

[ABOVE] At sunset on a summer evening in 2002, a Northern Plains Railroad grain train, which originated at Canadian Pacific's Thief River Falls Yard, is heading west through March toward the railroad's terminal at Fordville, North Dakota. At the time, train speeds were limited to ten miles per hour. Since then the track has been rebuilt with welded rail and speeds increased. Northern Plains leased the former Soo Line Wheat Lines west of Thief River Falls from Canadian Pacific in January 1997. Photograph by Andy Cummings.

[OPPOSITE, ABOVE] Ever wonder how all those railroad cars are loaded or unloaded? Railroads and their shippers handle the task in a variety of ways. At Alvarado, an operator at an elevator shoots grain into a waiting hopper car as a Northern Plains train approaches in September 2003. Photograph by Andy Cummings.

[OPPOSITE, BELOW] On the Iron Range, taconite plants use facilities such as this to load ore cars with taconite pellets. Trains crawl along at slow speeds, running directly through the loading facility without stopping. This is US Steel's Minntac Plant at Mountain Iron in November 1974. Minntac's loader could fill one car per minute. Photograph by James Kreuzberger.

[ABOVE] Once loaded, cars of taconite pellets must be moved to the dock or, in the case of raw taconite ore, to processing plants. Cliffs Northshore Mining moves raw taconite forty-seven miles from the mine at Babbitt to the processing plant at Silver Bay on Lake Superior over its former Reserve Mining line. A loaded ore train rolls east through a picturesque snow-covered landscape on Christmas Eve 2010. This location is at milepost 23.5, about halfway between Babbitt and Silver Bay. Photograph by David C. Schauer.

[OPPOSITE, ABOVE] After arrival in Silver Bay, Northshore uses a rotary dumper to unload cars. The mechanism holds the car to a section of track and rotates the track and car together to dump the contents. Cars used in this type of unloading are usually gondolas and hoppers equipped with special rotary couplers on one end. The dumper rotates the cars on the axis of the couplers. Cars must all be oriented the same way or the coupler will break when the dumper rotates. This is the rotary dumper at Northshore Mining in Silver Bay in 2010. Photograph by Shawn Christie.

[OPPOSITE, BELOW] Once the cars are unloaded, steel companies use lake boats to move taconite pellets to mills in the East and Midwest. On May 15, 2010, the one-thousand-foot *Walter J. McCarthy Jr.* is departing Silver Bay while railcars wait to be loaded with taconite tailings from the plant. This waste used to be dumped into Lake Superior, but in a landmark environmental case in the early 1970s, Reserve Mining was ordered to dispose of the tailings on land after they were found to contain traces of asbestos. Photograph by Shawn Christie.

[ABOVE] The traditional method of loading or unloading a boxcar is by forklift. This car of lumber is being unloaded at Progressive Rail's warehouse in Bloomington. At this warehouse shippers can pick up their shipment, store it, or have it trucked to them for final delivery. Photograph by Steve Glischinski.

[OPPOSITE, ABOVE] The Minnesota Northern Railroad was created in December 1996 when the railroad's former owner, short line conglomerate RailAmerica, purchased 204 miles of track from the Burlington Northern & Santa Fe. Included in the sale were 64 miles of trackage rights on Burlington Northern & Santa Fe from Crookston to Erskine and over Canadian Pacific from Erskine to Thief River Falls. Ownership of Minnesota Northern was turned over to KBN Incorporated and Independent Locomotive Service in 2001. They also co-own the St. Croix Valley Railroad based in Rush City. Minnesota Northern is based in Crookston. On September 2, 2009, a Minnesota Northern train crosses a field near Salol. This section of track has since been abandoned. Photograph by Steve Glischinski.

[OPPOSITE, BELOW] The sister railroad to Minnesota Northern is the St. Croix Valley, based in Rush City. The railroad operates thirty-six miles of former Northern Pacific track, and in a salute to its heritage, repainted its two locomotives in Northern Pacific colors with St. Croix Valley lettering. No. 1363 shows off its new paint as a mother and son take in the scene in Rush City on August 10, 2010. Photograph by Steve Glischinski.

[LEFT] Some railroads began to incorporate photographs in their employee timetables, such as this one issued by Wisconsin Central in 2000. The railroad would be purchased by Canadian National Railway the following year. Author's collection.

[ABOVE] Union Pacific operates three historic E9 passenger units to handle special trains. They once pulled the railroad's streamliners across the West. This photograph could easily be from the 1950s, but the date is June 14, 2007, as the crew changes on a Union Pacific special at Worthington. No. 949 was constructed by Electro-Motive in May 1955. Photograph by Steve Glischinski.

[OPPOSITE, ABOVE] Tunnels are relative rarities in Minnesota railroading. Surprisingly, there were five: on the Duluth, Winnipeg & Pacific near Duluth; Erie Mining Company in northeastern Minnesota; Northern Pacific and Soo Line tunnels at Westminster Street in St. Paul; and Soo Line's tunnel at its downtown Duluth station. The ex–Northern Pacific tunnel, constructed in 1885, is the only one still active. On December 3, 2006, engineer Jeff Terry is bringing a Canadian Pacific train west through the brick-lined ex–Northern Pacific tunnel. Canadian Pacific has operating rights over this BNSF line. The adjacent Soo Line tunnel was abandoned in 1978. Photograph by Jeff Terry.

[OPPOSITE, FAR RIGHT] On October 13, 1979, a northbound Duluth, Winnipeg & Pacific freight heads out of the north portal of their curved tunnel at milepost 7.4 outside Duluth. To gain access to Duluth, the railroad blasted a route out of the hills, constructing the tunnel and a shelf that allowed it to descend to Duluth on a 1.15 percent grade. The 520-foot rock tunnel through Ely's Peak and the line into Duluth were abandoned in 1984. The railroad moved to a new facility in Superior, Wisconsin, since the yard it used to interchange cars with other railroads was displaced by the extension of Interstate 35 through downtown Duluth. Photograph by Steve Glischinski.

[OPPOSITE, BELOW] The longest tunnel in the state is the 1,800-foot Cramer Tunnel on the former Erie Mining Company/LTV Steel railroad in northeastern Minnesota. It was constructed in 1955 and 1956 when Erie built a seventy-two-mile line between Hoyt Lakes and Taconite Harbor. On August 27, 1989, a loaded train bursts out of the tunnel heading to Taconite Harbor. The F9 locomotives, built in 1956, were among the last of their model in service, pulling trains until July 2001. In forty-three years of operation, these trains hauled loads totaling just over 300 million tons of taconite, operating eight hours a day, nine months a year. Photograph by Lori Van Oosbree.

[ABOVE] As passenger service wound down, many depots were recycled for other uses. One example is the Duluth, Winnipeg & Pacific passenger depot in Virginia. Located on Silver Lake, the three-story, orange sandstone and brick building was constructed by the Baily & Marsh Company in 1913. The woodwork on the ground floor was of oak hardwood; birch was used on the second level. Eleven chandeliers illuminated the interior. It saw its last passenger train on July 1, 1961. It was sold in the late 1970s, and today it is the home of the Northern State Bank of Virginia. Fishermen are seen dropping a line near the depot on June 5, 2011. Photograph by Todd Mavec.

[LEFT] The date is January 4, 2001, almost forty-four and a half years after the first crude ore was dumped into the crusher at Erie Mining Company's Hoyt Lakes taconite plant. At eighty-five tons per carload, just over one billion tons of taconite had been hauled to the crusher over the years. The plant, now owned by LTV Steel Mining Company, was being shut down as a result of LTV's bankruptcy. As the last train is shoved into the crusher building, a broom placed in the last car indicates that the mine has been swept clean and is being shut down. Photograph by Doug Buell.

[OPPOSITE] Duluth can be a busy place for watching both boats and trains in action. On May 22, 2006, a Duluth, Missabe & Iron Range Railway switch job spots ore cars on Dock 6. Across St. Louis Bay in Superior, Wisconsin, a Union Pacific coal train unloads coal at the Midwest Energy Resources Company terminal for shipment to Michigan. Traversing the bay is the *Cason J. Callaway,* arriving with limestone for unloading at the C. Reiss Coal Company dock. Canadian National Railway purchased the Duluth, Missabe & Iron Range in 2004; the acquisition included the US Steel Great Lakes Fleet. As a result, the Canadian-based railroad owns the ore docks, the dock train, and the boat in this photograph. Photograph by David C. Schauer.

[OPPOSITE] Minnesota never had true mountain railroading. The closest was Chicago Great Western's former Winona & Southwestern line to Winona, which included towering trestles and horseshoe curves near Bear Creek. It was abandoned in 1932, but a few miles south was Chicago & North Western's line that followed Garvin Brook through the Stockton Valley west of Minnesota City. Nearly 150 years after the Winona & St. Peter constructed the line, Dakota, Minnesota & Eastern train 486 is descending the grade through the valley. Photograph by John Leopard.

[ABOVE] Short line railroads continue to thrive in the twenty-first century. The Minnesota Southern Railway was formed in November 2001. The track is owned by the Buffalo Ridge Rail Authority and operated by Minnesota Southern under lease. It operates forty-one miles of track between Agate (near Worthington) and Manley that once belonged to the Omaha Road and Chicago & North Western. Among the commodities it carries are animal feed, ethanol, dried distillers grain, fertilizer, organic corn, and soybeans. Under a perfect autumn sky, a Minnesota Southern train rolls west near Magnolia on October 1, 2010. Photograph by John Leopard.

[LEFT, ABOVE] Another railroad created in the twenty-first century is the Northern Lines Railway. The company runs twenty-three miles of former Great Northern–Burlington Northern track in the St. Cloud area. It began operations on April 23, 2005. A Northern Lines train is crossing the Mississippi River heading to the yard in St. Cloud after switching industries on the east side of the city on September 15, 2006. The caboose is used as a platform for the crew to ride when making reverse movements. Photograph by Chris Laskowski.

[LEFT, BELOW] May 13, 2002, marked the end of former logging railroad Duluth & Northeastern when its name was changed to Cloquet Terminal Railroad. Its main purpose is to switch cars at the large Sappi Paper Mill in Cloquet. Until 2002 the mill was owned by Potlatch, but when it was sold to Sappi the railroad came with it. Sappi elected for legal reasons to change the name. A new red paint scheme came with the name change, modeled by engine 33 on July 16, 2007. No. 33 was constructed in 1941 and was still going strong more than sixty years later. Photograph by Steve Glischinski.

[OPPOSITE] For twenty-two years, the *Minnesota Zephyr* dinner train ran elegant dining trips in the Twin Cities area. It began operations in September 1986 as the *Minnetonka Zephyr* in Spring Park but moved to Stillwater and found a profitable niche for those seeking an unusual dining experience. The train had two domes and three table cars used for three-and-a-half-hour trips featuring five-course meals. On December 31, 2008, the train made its last run; its owner cited his desire to retire, a downturn in business, and a $1.6 million loss the previous two years. The *Zephyr* is heading out of Stillwater on November 11, 2007. Photograph by Steve Glischinski.

[ABOVE] An example of how marketing and customer service breed success can be found at Progressive Rail Inc. Beginning operations in 1996 at the Airlake Industrial Park in Lakeville, the railroad concentrated on customer service, setting up transloading facilities at Airlake and aggressively promoting rail service. Traffic grew, and the company made deals with Canadian Pacific and Union Pacific to operate lines in Bloomington, Eagan, Faribault, and on the Northfield–Lakeville and Northfield–Cannon Falls branches. It also runs railroads in Missouri and Wisconsin. On June 6, 2005, the Northfield–Lakeville turn is rolling north near Eureka Center. The locomotives are painted in a scheme reminiscent of the old Minneapolis, Northfield & Southern that once owned this track. Photograph by Steve Glischinski.

[LEFT] Progressive Rail's headquarters building at Airlake was constructed to look like an old railroad warehouse. The chimney includes this sign advising all to "ship by rail." Photograph by Steve Glischinski.

[RIGHT] With temperatures hovering around minus 15 degrees, even the locals have abandoned this bar in downtown South Haven as train 490 rolls across Main Street on January 10, 2009. Photograph by Jeff Terry.

[BELOW] Night on Canadian Pacific's former Soo Line route west of Minneapolis finds train 298 lighting up the night sky on Novermber 24, 2007. It is waiting to meet a fleet of westbound trains at Murray siding in Belgrade. Murray was named for longtime Soo Line president Leonard H. Murray. Photograph by Jeff Terry.

Beginning in 1995, Canadian Pacific Railway began buying locomotives from General Electric to modernize its fleet, a practice it continued into the twenty-first century. On June 20, 2002, Canadian Pacific 8604, a 4,400-horsepower General Electric model AC4400CW built the year before, passes the old Soo Line passenger depot in this view from the roof of an auto parts store. In 1994 and 1995 the City of Thief River Falls renovated and remodeled the depot to serve as the city hall. The remodeling preserved interior features such as the terrazzo floors and the wooden trim and doors in the passenger waiting area. Photograph by Andy Cummings.

Minnesota railroads rarely make big public relations splashes. One exception is Canadian Pacific Railway's *Holiday Train*. In December 1999, Canadian Pacific began running the train, decorated with thousands of Christmas lights, across Canada. Its mission is to collect food and money for local food banks and to raise awareness in the fight against hunger. In 2001 a second *Holiday Train* was launched in the United States. At each stop, the train provides a boxcar stage where a musical program is performed. Canadian Pacific makes a contribution to the local food bank and encourages visitors to donate food and funds. On December 12, 2007, the *Holiday Train* arrives at the Hastings depot. Photograph by Jeff Terry.

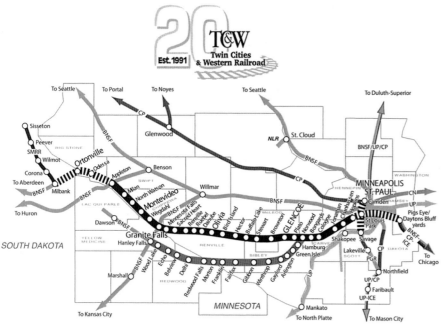

Twin Cities & Western Railroad System Map

▬▬▬▬	Twin Cities & Western
▬▬▬▬	Minnesota Prairie Line
|||||||||	Trackage rights

[ABOVE] Since 1985 a single Amtrak train, the Chicago–Seattle–Portland *Empire Builder,* has served Minnesota. The original *Empire Builder* entered service in 1929 for the Great Northern Railway and has been in continuous operation since. When Amtrak took over the service in 1971, it rerouted the train over the Milwaukee Road, rather than the Burlington Route, between St. Paul and Chicago. The classic Milwaukee Road logo is visible on the bridge at Hastings as the *Empire Builder* streaks west across the Mississippi River on July 13, 2010. Photograph by Jerry Huddleston.

[OPPOSITE] By the time Twin Cities & Western celebrated its twentieth anniversary in 2011, the short line had switched to a newer fleet of locomotives, rebuilt its track, and taken over operation of the line from Norwood to Hanley Falls through subsidiary Minnesota Prairie Line. On October 15, 2010, Twin Cities & Western's *Reubel Turn,* which operates between Glencoe and the Southern Minnesota Sugar Beet Cooperative near Renville, heads west through Bird Island past autumn flowers and pumpkins. Photograph by Steve Glischinski.

[LEFT] In July 2011, the Twin Cities & Western operated a series of excursion trips to celebrate its twentieth anniversary and produced a special souvenir booklet with this map for riders. Author's collection.

The last main line steam power operating on a regular basis made its final runs in 1960. Over forty years later, big steam locomotives still run in Minnesota, albeit only occasionally. Union Pacific has maintained a steam excursion program since 1960. After it purchased the Chicago & North Western in 1995, Union Pacific steam made sporadic Minnesota visits. No. 3985, a 4-6-6-4 Challenger type and the world's largest operating steam locomotive, is crossing the Mississippi River on the former Milwaukee Road–Omaha Road bridge in Lilydale on September 30, 2008. Photograph by Steve Glischinski.

Canadian Pacific Railway established a steam locomotive program of its own in 2001. It restored Hudson-type 4-6-4 No. 2816, built by Montreal Locomotive Works in December 1930. The engine, based in Calgary, Alberta, serves as a goodwill ambassador for the railway and occasionally makes forays into the United States. On September 6, 2007, No. 2816 is crossing the St. Croix River from Minnesota into Wisconsin with a special photo train organized by the author. Photograph by Steve Glischinski.

[OPPOSITE, ABOVE] Minneapolis-based Milwaukee Road 4-8-4 No. 261 makes regular steam excursion trips in Minnesota. Operated by the non-profit Friends of the 261, the locomotive was restored to service in 1993 after more than three decades of display at the National Railroad Museum in Green Bay, Wisconsin. Night in Glencoe finds 261 posing for photographs along with Milwaukee Road Skytop observation car *Cedar Rapids*, built in 1948 at the Milwaukee shops. Lerro Productions organized the special photo session on May 9, 2008. Photograph by Steve Glischinski.

[OPPOSITE, BELOW] Back on the original Milwaukee Road track that it traveled in regular service between 1944 and 1954, No. 261 is pulling a special freight train on the Twin Cities & Western. The train is getting a highball signal at the Buffalo Lake depot on a rainy May 10, 2008, during a photo charter organized by Lerro Productions. Photograph by Steve Glischinski.

[ABOVE] Another steam locomotive came to Minnesota in 2007. Soo Line 4-6-2 No. 2719, built in 1923, made the last steam run on the Soo in 1959 and then retired to Carson Park in Eau Claire, Wisconsin. The Locomotive & Tower Preservation Fund of Eau Claire restored it in 1998. By 2007 rising insurance rates and a lack of cooperative railroads left the engine with nowhere to operate. It was leased to the Lake Superior Railroad Museum for operation on the North Shore Scenic Railroad between Duluth and Two Harbors. On September 9, 2007, the engine poses at Two Harbors as a Canadian National ore train heads north. No. 2719 wears a nameplate for the Mountaineer, a passenger train it pulled in the 1920s. Photograph by Steve Glischinski.

[ABOVE] When blizzards bring their worst, the final line of defense for railroads is the rotary snowplow. Slow moving, prone to breakdowns, and expensive to run, they are called to duty only as a last resort. On February 7, 2011, BNSF Railway has brought out a former Northern Pacific rotary to clear the branch from Appleton, Minnesota, to Watertown, South Dakota. Here it is chewing through a drift at Nassau, Minnesota. The next day the rotary suffered a catastrophic failure when some of its blades broke off and were thrown well off the right-of-way. Photograph by Steve Glischinski.

[OPPOSITE, ABOVE] For decades advocates hoped to establish commuter rail service in the Twin Cities area, but the idea didn't gain any traction until officials in Anoka County pushed for it. In 1997 the county formed the Northwest Corridor Development Authority, which succeeded in persuading the legislature and the federal government to fund the Northstar Commuter Rail Line. Construction began in 2007 to build stations and upgrade signals and track over forty miles of BNSF Railway from downtown Minneapolis to Big Lake. On April 15, 2010, a Northstar train crosses the Mississippi River leaving downtown Minneapolis. Photograph by Steve Glischinski.

[OPPOSITE, BELOW] One advantage of rail transportation is that trains run regardless of the weather. In Minnesota, with its rugged winter weather, Northstar trains can keep moving as road traffic snarls. A westbound train rolls through a snow-covered landscape in Coon Rapids in December 2010. Photograph by Steve Glischinski.

[OPPOSITE, FAR RIGHT] On the first day of Northstar service, November 16, 2009, conductor Vincent Roberts welcomes passengers aboard at the Big Lake station. Photograph by Steve Glischinski.

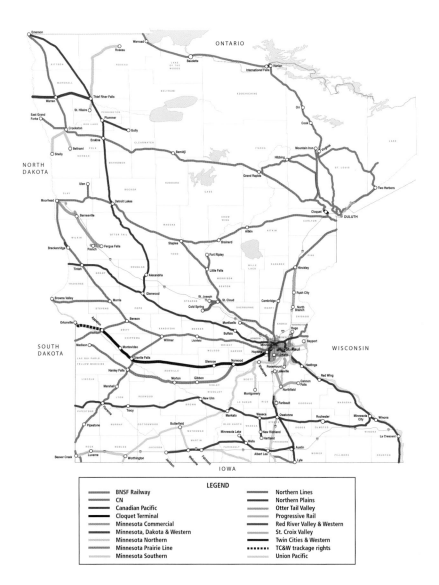

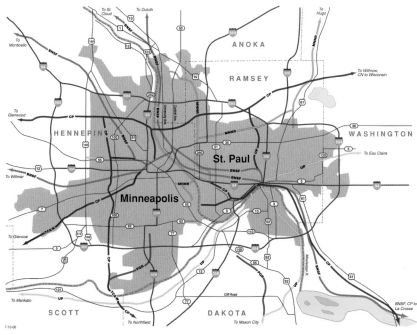

In 2011, there were seventeen freight railroads operating in the state, plus the North Shore Scenic tourist railroad between Duluth and Two Harbors. Not shown is Cliffs Northshore Mining's private industrial railroad between Babbitt and Silver Bay. Maps by Briggs Business Communication.

LEGEND

- BNSF Railway
- CN
- Canadian Pacific
- Cloquet Terminal
- Minnesota Commercial
- Minnesota, Dakota & Western
- Minnesota Northern
- Minnesota Prairie Line
- Minnesota Southern
- Northern Lines
- Northern Plains
- Otter Tail Valley
- Progressive Rail
- Red River Valley & Western
- St. Croix Valley
- Twin Cities & Western
- TC&W trackage rights
- Union Pacific

Duluth, Missabe & Iron Range ore cars are enveloped in steam at sunset on March 27, 2011. The old cars, approaching sixty years of service, are running out their last miles. Missabe Road owner Canadian National was buying new replacement cars and sweeping away the older rolling stock, exemplifying the ever-changing nature of Minnesota railroading in the twenty-first century. Photograph by Steve Glischinski.

On May 27, 2007, Amtrak's *Empire Builder* passes the closed concourse of the St. Paul Union Depot on its way to Chicago. In January 2011, a $243 million renovation was begun that will return trains to the station. The building will be shared with Metro Transit, Jefferson Lines buses, future commuter rail lines, and a possible high-speed rail line to Chicago.

Central Corridor Light Rail trains will stop in front of the depot when the line is completed in 2014. When the Union Depot reopens, Minnesota passenger railroading will have come full circle, returning to a building that once represented the heart of railroading in Minnesota. Photograph by Steve Glischinski.

Minnesota Railroads

1940 and 2012

1940
(excludes small industrial lines and street railways)

Chicago, Burlington & Quincy Railroad (Burlington Route)

Chicago & North Western System

Chicago Great Western Railway

Chicago, Milwaukee, St. Paul & Pacific Railroad (Milwaukee Road)

Chicago, Rock Island & Pacific Railroad (Rock Island)

Chicago, St. Paul, Minneapolis & Omaha Railway (Omaha Road)

Chicago, St. Paul, Minneapolis & Sault Ste. Marie Railway (Soo Line)

Duluth & Northeastern Railroad

Duluth, Missabe & Iron Range Railway

Duluth, Winnipeg & Pacific Railway

Duluth Union Depot & Transfer Co. (controlled by Northern Pacific)

Great Northern Railway

Green Bay & Western Railroad

Illinois Central Railroad

Minneapolis & St. Louis Railway

Minneapolis, Anoka & Cuyuna Range Railroad

Minneapolis Eastern Railway

Minneapolis, Northfield & Southern Railway

Minnesota & International Railway

Minnesota & Manitoba Railroad (Canadian National Railway)

Minnesota, Dakota & Western Railway

Minnesota Northwestern Electric Railway (abandoned 1940)

Minnesota Transfer Railway

Minnesota Western Railroad

Northern Pacific Railway

St. Paul Bridge & Terminal Railway

St. Paul Union Depot Company

Winona Bridge Railway

MINNESOTA RAILROADS IN 1940 AND 2012

2012

BNSF Railway
Canadian National Railway
Canadian Pacific Railway
Cloquet Terminal Railroad
Dakota, Minnesota & Eastern Railroad (owned by Canadian Pacific)
Minnesota Commercial Railway
Minnesota, Dakota & Western Railway
Minnesota Northern Railroad
Minnesota Prairie Line (owned by Twin Cities & Western)
Minnesota Southern Railway

North Shore Scenic Railroad
Northern Lines Railway
Northern Plains Railroad
NorthShore Mining (private industrial)
Otter Tail Valley Railroad
Progressive Rail, Inc.
Red River Valley & Western Railroad
St. Croix Valley Railroad
Twin Cities & Western Railroad
Union Pacific Railroad

Notes

1. AN INDUSTRY IN TRANSITION, 1940–1960

1. Great Northern Railway Company, 1941 annual report, 3.
2. Minnesota Railroad and Warehouse Commission annual reports, 1940, 1945.
3. Hilton, *Amtrak,* 2.
4. EuDaly et al., *The Complete Book of North American Railroading,* 64.
5. Frailey, *Twilight of the Great Trains,* 5.
6. Lester, "Freight Houses," 474.
7. *Streamliners: America's Lost Trains.*
8. Olson, *The Electric Railways of Minnesota,* 504.
9. Morgan, "The Diesel That Did It."
10. Morgan, "The Pure Railroad," 23.
11. Ibid.

2. THE STRUGGLE FOR SURVIVAL, 1960–1980

1. Blaszak, "Free to Compete," 27.
2. Edmonson, *Journey to Amtrak,* 8–11.
3. Amtrak news release, "Amtrak Sets New Ridership Record," October 11, 2010.
4. Mortenson Construction news release, "Mortenson Breaks Ground on the Union Depot in St. Paul, MN," January 18, 2011.
5. Edmonson, *Journey to Amtrak,* 99.
6. *Amtrak System Passenger Timetable,* November 14, 1971, 62, 66.
7. Discussion of the Duluth service in this section is taken primarily from Glischinski, "Nine Lives of the North Star."
8. EuDaly et al., *Complete Book of North American Railroading,* 66.
9. Ibid.
10. Blaszak, "Free to Compete," 27.
11. Grant, *The North Western,* 220.
12. Blaszak, "Free to Compete," 26–27.
13. Drury, *Historical Guide to North American Railroads,* 91.
14. Blaszak, "Free to Compete," 27.
15. Grant, *The Corn Belt Route,* 176–80.
16. Glischinski, *Burlington Northern and Its Heritage,* 57–61.
17. "The Biggest Bankruptcy Ever."
18. Solomon, "Consolidated Rail Corp. (Conrail)," 333.
19. Drury, *Historical Guide to North American Railroads,* 84, 91.
20. Ibid.
21. Grant, *The North Western,* 232.
22. Glischinski, "Reversal of Fortunes, 1950–2005," 72–73.
23. Glischinski, *Burlington Northern and Its Heritage,* 66.
24. Phillips, "Bob Downing Deserves His Place in History Books."
25. Glischinski, *Burlington Northern and Its Heritage,* 66.
26. Glischinski, "The Train That Started It All."
27. Glischinski, *Burlington Northern and Its Heritage,* 72.

NOTES

3. REVIVAL AND REHABILITATION, 1980–2000

1. Blaszak, "Free to Compete."
2. Glischinski, *Burlington Northern and Its Heritage,* 87–88.
3. Ibid., 88.
4. Ibid., 96.
5. Ibid., 98.
6. EuDaly et al., *Complete Book of North American Railroading,* 79.
7. Cummings and Huddleston, *Dakota, Minnesota & Eastern,* 47.
8. Glischinski, "Coming: A Third Powder River Basin Player," 10–11.
9. Bleizeffer, "Feds Reject Railroad Loan."
10. Scribbins, *The Milwaukee Road, 1928–1985,* 202–3.
11. Ibid., 88.
12. Glischinski, *Regional Railroads of the Midwest,* 137.
13. Easton, "Soo News," October 1989; January 1990.
14. Easton, "Soo News," January 1990, 4.
15. Glischinski, *Regional Railroads of the Midwest,* 124.
16. Ibid., 125.
17. Ibid., 125–29.
18. Ibid., 61.
19. Association of American Railroads, *An Overview of America's Freight Railroads,* April 2011.
20. EuDaly et al., *Complete Book of North American Railroading,* 74–75.
21. Ibid., 74.
22. Positively Minnesota, Minnesota Department of Employment and Economic Development Web site, http://www.positivelyminnesota.com.
23. EuDaly et al., *Complete Book of North American Railroading,* 77–79.
24. Ibid., 78–79.
25. Hoback, "Coal and Railroads."
26. Lester, "Bulk-Commodity Terminals."
27. Association of American Railroads, *Overview of America's Freight Railroads,* May 2008.
28. McGonigal, "End-of-Train Devices."

4. RAILROADING IN THE TWENTY-FIRST CENTURY

1. Barken, *Railroad Transportation Energy Efficiency.*
2. "Railroads Chugging Hard to Anticipate Demand, Add Track," *Lincoln (Neb.) Journal-Star,* May 17, 2011.
3. Association of American Railroads, *An Overview of America's Freight Railroads,* April 2011.
4. Barken, *Railroad Transportation Energy Efficiency.*
5. Association of American Railroads, *An Overview of America's Freight Railroads,* April 2011.
6. BNSF Railway news release, November 3, 2009.
7. CBC Business News, April 25, 2011, http://www.cbc.ca/news/business/story/2011/04/25/gates-cn-railway-shareholder.html.
8. Positively Minnesota, Minnesota Department of Employment and Economic Development Web site, http://www.positivelyminnesota.com.
9. Glischinski, "Minnesota's Rail Service Prepares to Shine."
10. Association of American Railroads, *An Overview of America's Freight Railroads,* April 2011.
11. The statistics for 2009 are the most recent that are available. Association of American Railroads, U.S. Freight Railroad Industry Snapshot, http://www.aar.org/KeyIssues/Railroads-States.aspx.

Bibliography

Abbey, Wallace W. *The Little Jewel.* Pueblo, Colo.: Pinon Publications, 1984.

Association of American Railroads. *An Overview of America's Freight Railroads.* Washington, D.C.: Association of American Railroads, May 2008.

———. *An Overview of America's Freight Railroads.* Washington, D.C.: Association of American Railroads, April 2011.

Barken, Chris. *Railroad Transportation Energy Efficiency.* Railroad Engineering Program, University of Illinois at Urbana–Champaign, 2009. http://www.istc.illinois.edu.

"The Biggest Bankruptcy Ever." *Time Magazine,* July 6, 1970.

Blaszak, Michael W. "Free to Compete." *Trains Magazine,* October 2010, 24–33.

Bleizeffer, Dustin. "Feds Reject Railroad Loan." *Casper Star Tribune,* February 27, 2007.

Cummings, Andy, and Jerry Huddleston. *Dakota, Minnesota & Eastern: A Modern Granger Railroad.* David City, Neb.: South Platte Press, 2005.

Drury, George H. *The Historical Guide to North American Railroads.* Waukesha, Wis.: Kalmbach Publishing, 1991.

Easton, Larry, ed. "Soo News." *Soo, the Magazine of the Soo Line Historical and Technical Society,* October 1989, 4–5; January 1990, 4–5.

Edmonson, Harold A. *Journey to Amtrak: The Year History Rode the Passenger Train.* Milwaukee: Kalmbach Publishing, 1972.

EuDaly, Kevin, et al. *The Complete Book of North American Railroading.* Minneapolis: Voyageur Press, 2009.

Frailey, Fred W. *Twilight of the Great Trains.* Waukesha, Wis.: Kalmbach Publishing, 1998.

Frey, Robert L., and Lorenz P. Schrenk. *Northern Pacific Diesel Era, 1945–1970.* San Marino, Calif.: Golden West Books, 1988.

———. *Northern Pacific Supersteam Era, 1925–1945.* San Marino, Calif.: Golden West Books, 1985.

Glischinski, Steve. *Burlington Northern and Its Heritage.* Andover, N.J.: Andover Junction Publications, 1992.

———. "Coming: A Third Powder River Basin Player." *Trains Magazine,* February 2002, 10–11.

———. "Going Out (and Back) for Dinner." *Trains Magazine,* June 1990.

———. "Minnesota's Rail Service Prepares to Shine," *Passenger Train Journal,* Fourth Quarter, 2009.

———. "Minntac Rail Operations." *Missabe Road Historical Society Ore Extra* 14, no. 4 (Spring 2002).

———. "Nine Lives of the Northstar." *Passenger Train Journal,* May–June 1985, 16–23, 38.

———. *Regional Railroads of the Midwest.* Minneapolis: Voyageur Press, 2007.

———. "Reversal of Fortunes, 1950–2005." In EuDaly et al., *The Complete Book of North American Railroading.* Minneapolis: Voyageur Press, 2009.

———. "The Train That Started It All." *Trains Magazine,* March 2011, 54–55.

Grant, H. Roger. *The Corn Belt Route: A History of the Chicago Great Western Railroad Company.* DeKalb: Northern Illinois University Press, 1984.

———. *The North Western: A History of the Chicago & North Western Railway System.* DeKalb: Northern Illinois University Press, 1996.

Great Northern Railway Company. *Statistical Supplement to the 68th Annual Report.* 1956.

BIBLIOGRAPHY

——. *Statistical Supplement to the 70th Annual Report.* 1958.

——. *Talking It Over* 10, no. 8 (August 1967).

Green, Gene. *Minneapolis & St. Louis in Color.* Kutztown, Penn.: Morning Sun Books, 1996.

Hilton, George W. *Amtrak: The National Railroad Passenger Corporation.* Washington, D.C.: American Enterprise Institute for Public Policy Research, 1980.

Hoback, Thomas. "Coal and Railroads." In *Encyclopedia of North American Railroads,* 294–95. Bloomington: Indiana University Press, 2007.

Kuebler, William R., Jr. *The Vista Dome North Coast Limited.* Hamilton, Mont.: Oso Publishing, 2004.

Lester, David C. "Bulk-Commodity Terminals." In *Encyclopedia of North American Railroads,* 474. Bloomington: Indiana University Press, 2007.

——. "Freight Houses." In *Encyclopedia of North American Railroads,* 474. Bloomington: Indiana University Press, 2007.

Lewis, Edward A. *American Shortline Railway Guide.* 4th ed. Waukesha, Wis.: Kalmbach Publishing, 1991.

Loving, Rush, Jr. *The Men Who Loved Trains: The Story of Men Who Battled Greed to Save an Ailing Industry.* Bloomington: Indiana University Press, 2006.

Luecke, John C. *The Great Northern in Minnesota: The Foundations of an Empire.* St. Paul: Grenadier Publications, 1997.

Luecke, John C. *Dreams, Disasters, and Demise: The Milwaukee Road in Minnesota.* St. Paul: Grenadier Publications, 1988.

Mailer, Stan. *The Omaha Road: Chicago, St. Paul, Minneapolis & Omaha.* Mukilteo, Wash.: Hundman Publishing, 2004.

Mailer, Stanley H. "Before the Dragon." *Railfan & Railroad,* September 1982, 45.

McCreary, Charles B. *Train Pictures: A Railfan's Memoir, 1946–1957.* Minneapolis: Malabar Rails Publishing, 2011.

McGonigal, Robert S. "End-of-Train Devices." *Trains Magazine,* May 2006.

Middleton, William D. *The Railroad Scene.* San Marino, Calif.: Golden West Books, 1969.

Morgan, David P. "The Diesel That Did It." *Trains Magazine,* February 1960.

——. "The Pure Railroad." *Trains Magazine,* January 1969, 20–25.

Nelson, Andrew S. *Green Bay & Western Color Pictorial.* La Mirada, Calif.: Four Ways West Publications, 2003.

Olson, Russell L. *The Electric Railways of Minnesota.* Hopkins: Minnesota Transportation Museum, 1976.

Phillips, Don, "Bob Downing Deserves His Place in History Books," *Trains Magazine,* January 2011, 10–11.

Schauer, David C. *Duluth, Missabe & Iron Range Railway in Color.* Kutztown, Penn.: Morning Sun Books, 2002.

Scribbins, Jim. *The Milwaukee Road, 1928–1985.* Forest Park, Ill.: Heimburger House Publishing, 2001.

Soloman, Brian. "Consolidated Rail Corp. (Conrail)." In *Encyclopedia of North American Railroads,* 333. Bloomington: Indiana University Press, 2007.

Stagner, Lloyd E. *Burlington Route Steam Finale.* David City, Neb.: South Platte Press, 1997.

Stout, Greg. *Route of the Rockets: Rock Island in the Streamlined Era.* Hart, Mo.: White River Productions, 1997.

Strauss, John F., Jr. *Great Northern Pictorial.* Vol. 3. La Mirada, Calif.: Four Ways West Publications, 1993.

——. *Northern Pacific Pictorial.* Vol. 4. La Mirada, Calif.: Four Ways West Publications, 2000.

Streamliners: America's Lost Trains, PBS Television, 2001.

Thompson, Richard E., and Steven J. Monson. *The Taylors Falls & Lake Superior Railroad.* Chisago City, Minn.: Iron Horse Central Railroad Museum, 2005.

Wood, Charles, and Dorothy Wood. *The Great Northern Railway: A Pictorial Study.* Edmonds, Wash.: Pacific Fast Mail, 1979.

Index

INDEX

Big Boy steam locomotives (Union Pacific Railroad), 203
Big Lake, Minnesota, 245, 274
Big Sky Blue colors (Great Northern Railway), 119, 212
Big Sky Mine (Montana), 104
Big Stone Lake (Minnesota), 35
Bird Island, Minnesota, 268
Blackfeet Indians, 19
Black Hawk (Burlington Route passenger train), xvi, 6
Bloom, Al (Milwaukee Road locomotive engineer), 126
Bloomington, Minnesota, 209, 254, 264
BNSF Railway, 89, 93, 202, 203, 204, 230, 233, 238, 240, 242, 243, 244, 245, 246, 248, 249, 254, 256, 274, 280; purchased by Berkshire Hathaway Inc., 244. *See also* Atchison, Topeka & Santa Fe Railway; Burlington Northern
Boise, Idaho, 245
Boise Cascade Corporation, 229
Bombardier Inc., 245
Boom Island (Minneapolis), 47
Boston, Massachusetts, 105
Brainerd, Minnesota, 4, 36, 60, 67, 147, 162, 193, 214, 216
Brainerd Shops (Northern Pacific), 36, 60, 87
brakeman, 94
Breckenridge, Minnesota, 24, 28, 100, 157, 200
Bridge 15 (Lilydale, Minnesota), 48, 49
Brook Park, Minnesota, 117, 145, 233, 240
Brooten Line (Soo Line), 168, 170
Brotherhood of Locomotive Firemen and Enginemen, 44
Brotherhood of Railway and Airline Clerks, 103
Brownsville, Minnesota, 241
Budd, John (Great Northern Railway president), 114
Buffalo, Minnesota, 168
Buffalo Lake, Minnesota, 273
Buffalo Ridge, 248
Buffalo Ridge Rail Authority, 244, 261. *See also* Minnesota Southern Railway
Buffett, Warren, 242, 244. *See also* BNSF Railway
Burger, Chris, 222
Burkhardt, Ed, 222
Burlington, Iowa, 8
Burlington Northern, xiii, 19, 31, 81, 100, 102–3, 104, 105, 106, 119, 145, 147, 149, 152, 155, 158, 162, 164, 166, 189, 197, 199–200, 202, 203, 204, 214, 216, 219, 222, 226, 230, 236, 238, 240, 244, 262; Cascade Green colors, 119, 145; Robert W. Downing, 104; headquarters leaves St. Paul, 199; Hutchinson Branch, 197, 200; Louis W. Menk (president), 104, 199; merger of Chicago, Burlington & Quincy, Great Northern, Northern Pacific and Spokane, Portland & Seattle, xiii–xiv, 102–3, 145; merger with Atchison, Topeka & Santa Fe Railway, 202, 238, 240; passenger service, 147, 149. *See also* BNSF Railway
Burlington Northern & Santa Fe Railway. *See* BNSF Railway
Burlington Route (Chicago, Burlington & Quincy Railroad), xiii, xvi, 2, 6, 8, 18, 29, 39, 85, 88, 99, 100, 102–3, 136, 141, 145, 152, 191, 202, 213, 219, 245, 268, 279; merger with Great Northern, Northern Pacific and Spokane, Portland & Seattle, xiii–xiv, 102–3, 145; Winona Bridge Railway Company (owned with Green Bay & Western), 213, 279. *See also* Burlington Northern
Burlington Route passenger trains: *Afternoon Zephyr,* 39, 150, *Black Hawk,* xvi, 6, *Empire Builder,* 2, 29; *Twin Zephyrs,* 2, 39, 150; *Zephyr Rocket,* 8;
Burnsville, Minnesota, 105, 203

caboose, 204, 216
Caledonia, Minnesota, 176
Calgary, Alberta, 271
California, 117, 145
Calumet, Minnesota, 67
Cambridge, Minnesota, 101
Canada, 117, 180, 230, 245, 258, 267
Canadian National Railway(s), 65, 83, 100, 101, 110, 180, 194, 201, 206, 230, 244, 246, 254, 258, 273, 278, 280; buys Duluth, Missabe & Iron Range Railway, 244, 258; buys Wisconsin Central Ltd., 201, 244, 254; Minnesota & Manitoba Railroad, 279
Canadian Pacific Railway, 48, 70, 89, 90, 108, 124, 191, 200, 201, 202, 204, 218, 222, 224, 229, 232, 241, 243, 244, 246, 250, 254, 256, 264, 265–67, 271, 280; buys Dakota, Minnesota & Eastern and Iowa, Chicago & Eastern Railroads, 200, 224, 241, 244; buys outstanding stock of Soo Line, 124, 201, 204, 229; *Holiday Train,* 267; leases lines to Northern Plains Railroad, 218, 250; leases lines to Progressive Rail Inc., 244, 264; Murray siding, 265; sells lines to I&M Rail Link, 202, 241; sells lines to Twin Cities & Western, 201–2, 232; steam program, 271

INDEX

STEVE GLISCHINSKI began taking photographs of railroads in 1970 at the age of thirteen. Since then, his photographs of railroads in action have been published in many books and magazines. He is a correspondent for *Trains Magazine* and organizes railroad photography charter trips and the Railfan Weekend at the Lake Superior Railroad Museum. He is the author of several books on railroading and lives in Shoreview, Minnesota.

Also Published by the

University of Minnesota Press